Zen and the Art
of Resource Editing

We would like to thank the following for their assistance, without which this book would not be the same:

Our authors: **Jens Peter Alfke, Tom Chavez, Chris Holmes, Lisa Lee, Brendan McCarthy, Leonard Morgenstern, Brian Novack, Blaise R. Pabón, Rick Reynolds, Cliff Stoll, James W. Walker,** and **Steve Yaste**, without whom we wouldn't have a book.

Gray Shaw for lending his extraordinary editing skills through all editions of this book.

Tim Holmes, Wendy Masri, Tim Bodine and **Raines Cohen** for editing previous editions.

Tigran Johnson and **Phoenix Reed** for helping out in the last day rush.

Cliff Stoll for his enthusiasm and advice.

The Berkeley Public Library for letting us know who started Zen Buddhism, and the Buddha's real name.

Wendy Masri for her assistance with the custom lettering in the title on the cover.

Gary Little for keeping us informed about potential changes in *ResEdit* so that we could make sure we would be prepared.

FM Waves for their generous donation of custom clip art which is used throughout the book in the headers and introduction pages.

Utopia Grokware for their assistance and the donation of their services, as well as the screen shot of Flowfazer which is used in the background of the cover.

Robert Lettieri for his input on the page design.

And all the people who were enthusiastic about the previous editions, without which the third edition might not have been done.

Zen and the Art of Resource Editing

The BMUG Guide to ResEdit
Third Edition

Edited by

Derrick Schneider
Hans Hansen
Noah Potkin

Bhagabooks
Berkeley, California

Peachpit Press
Berkeley, California

Copyrights & Disclaimers:

Zen and the Art of Resource Editing, Third Edition:
The BMUG Guide to ResEdit.
Copyright © 1992 by Derrick Schneider, Hans Hansen, Noah Potkin
Printed in the United States of America.
ISBN: 0-938151-75-4

BMUG, Inc. is a 501(c)3 non-profit educational corporation. The mailing address is: 1442A Walnut St. #62, Berkeley, CA 94709. Telephone 510-549-2684. FAX 510-849-9026.

Flowfazer is a Macintosh product and is available from Utopia Grokware, 300 Valley Street, Suite 204, Sausalito, CA 94965. Telephone 415-331-0714.

The PostScript illustrations used throughout this book are Copyright FM Waves, 1991. FM Waves is located at 70 Derby Alley, San Francisco, CA 94115. Telephone 415-474-2752.

Limits of liability and disclaimer of warranty:

95 94 93 92   5 4 3 2 1

Dedicated to:

Rony Sebok & Steve Capps
who first brought us *ResEdit*

and

Siddhartha Gautauma & Bodhidharma
who first brought us Zen

Contents

Foreword

by Cliff Stoll

When I got ahold of the first edition of this book, I hadn't played with *ResEdit* in ages. I had some old version which I rarely used, and I had little idea of what I could do with it. I had never taken the time to sit down and learn it, since there were no instructions.

I was in the Bay Area for a while, so I stopped in at a BMUG meeting and picked up a copy of the book. I took it home that night and began to play with it. Gadzooks! I had never known that any of this could be possible! Reading through this book, I spent that entire night modifying my menus, changing my Trash, and editing dialogs to say all sorts of properly cool things.

The really wild thing about *ResEdit* is that you can use it on any Mac program. Just zap your resources here and there, and all of a sudden your Mac is really *your* Mac—an extension of your personality. Since everything about the

Mac—the sounds, the fonts, and a zillion other things— lives within a resource, *ResEdit* can tailor those resources to meet your needs. Of course, you need to tell it what to do.

However, this is not a book to read casually. You won't learn anything by curling up with a homespun quilt next to a roaring fire and reading through this book. You've got to abandon the family for a day or so, roll up your sleeves, lock yourself in your computer room, and get your keyboard dirty. Sit down with *ResEdit*, which comes with the book, turn to Chapter One, and just start hacking away. The chapters will tell you how to do the basic stuff, and then will give you a few ideas about other possible uses. However, there's nothing stopping you from going off and trying your own wild ideas or exploring. Poke around a little—you'll learn oodles about the way your Mac works. When you finally come out of your locked room into the light of day, you'll have a working knowledge of *ResEdit* which you can apply for as long as you've got your Mac.

Interestingly enough, there has been absolutely no information about using this program. ResEdit has been around almost as long as the Mac, but it seems as if no one really knew how to use it except programmers. As usual, BMUG has come through with a way of making the mysteries of the Mac seem easy to everyone. It doesn't surprise me that BMUG has come out with such a cool product, since cool is what they're all about.

Zen & the Art of Resource Editing

Preface

It's been more than a year since the idea of doing a BMUG *ResEdit* book was suggested to Derrick by one of BMUG's regulars. The idea stuck, and the book was soon underway. Derrick enlisted a variety of people from around BMUG to write sections on specific resource types. Hans and Noah joined in transforming it from a disorganized hodgepodge of files into a real book. Through the various problems we encountered, ranging from an early lack of authors to budgetary and political concerns, we were able to rush out the book to meet our deadline of the January 1991 Macworld Expo. Our goals for sales at Expo were conservative; 400 books sold would cover costs, and BMUG would have gotten its money back from the venture. Our actual results were suprising ; close to 1000 *Zen* books were sold in those four days. This success was even more surprising when we compared our thin book to Addison-Wesley's huge *ResEdit Complete*, being sold around the corner. It was then that we realized that not only did *ResEdit* and the book have an audience, but BMUG had one too. The book was so successful that we immediately began planning the second edition.

For the second edition, each of us had goals for how the book would look and read. Derrick was intent on cramming in as much stuff as possible, including information on the as yet unreleased *System 7* for which *ResEdit 2.1* was designed. Hans and Noah wanted to completely redesign the problematic layout and cover from scratch. We all wanted to surpass the first edition, and we did.

The second edition was more than twice the size, but more importantly, it was easier to read and more organized. It focused more on the practical aspects of *ResEdit*, including some neat things you could do with the just-released *System 7*. This book too, surprised us with its success, selling about 3,500 copies with little or no advertising out of the BMUG office and at the 1991 Boston Macworld Expo. While we were contemplating what we would add to the third printing, Peachpit Press became interested in distributing the book. So, we stopped contemplating and started doing, and the end result is what you are now holding. It has more information about new add-on editors and system tricks than the second edition and covers the stuff we had wanted to talk about, but that never made it to the printer. There are also a lot of "bug fixes" such as grammatical changes, the inevitable typos, and the dreaded technical errors.

One thing that all the editions have had in common is a drive to educate. People have always been scared of using *ResEdit*, since there weren't any instructions but only vague rumors about whole hard drives having been destroyed by this program. These fears are unfounded. A person using *ResEdit* knowledgeably (which this book will teach you how to do) won't do any damage. Even a severe error will not destroy your hard drive. As long as you use common sense, and this book, you'll find that *ResEdit* will quickly become one of your favorite utilities.

It is a love of Macintosh that we, the authors, designers, and editors of this book would like to impart to you. We all believe that useful information should not be withheld, or held in the hands of a select few. Users should understand their Macintoshes and work with them more efficiently as a result. In essence, information is everyone's right.

As noble as that belief sounds, it is not original. In fact, it is the driving force behind BMUG. Our slogan, in fact, is: "We are in the business of giving away information." It is this motive which gives us the drive to continually put out a 400-page, semiannual newsletter. While most newsletters might contain information about company picnics or whatever, our newsletter informs you about technical and political topics, answers your most frequent questions, and always teaches you something you don't know. It is in that same spirit that three BMUGers produced a book to inform the public about using *ResEdit*. We could not have produced this book without BMUG's willingness to promote it. Certainly the funding was important, but it was even more important to have BMUG's belief in the book—not just because it would make some money, (very few people thought it would to begin with) but because our book could only benefit from being presented by an organization that was built on a reputation of helping people. If you haven't looked into BMUG, we'd like to suggest that you do. For more information about BMUG, read the last appendix in this book or call our business office at (510) 549-2684. We'll be glad to send you some additional information about the group.

Derrick Schneider
Hans Hansen
Noah Potkin

Introduction

by Derrick Schneider

If you're a complete neophyte in the *ResEdit* world, you might be wondering why you should use *ResEdit*. You may have heard tales of its ability to bring down entire hard drives with a single mouse click, or something similar. Why take a risk like that? Well, to start with, those scary stories just aren't true. The real reason to use *ResEdit* lies at the heart of the Macintosh itself. As Mac users, most of us appreciate the ability we have to customize the Mac to our needs. We can change keyboard or mouse speeds, change our background patterns, or even "view by" however we want to. If we don't like the way Apple does something, we can change it, either in the Control Panel or in the Finder menus. *ResEdit* extends this ability to a grand scale. With *ResEdit*, if you don't like an icon, you can just change it. If you want a new sound, you can use *ResEdit* to install it. If you want a whole new keyboard layout, just change it with *ResEdit*. Don't just work on your Mac, make it work the way you it want to! Incidentally, I've never heard of someone erasing their hard drive with *ResEdit*, so I wouldn't be too worried about it. If you pay attention to what you're doing and don't recklessly delete resources or anything like that, you'll be fine.

When I started this book, I had to tell the authors who our audience was. This is important, because *ResEdit* was designed as a tool for developers who write programs on the Macintosh, but this book was not aimed at developers. *ResEdit* gives one the power to quickly create the resources which are so common among Macintosh applications—which in fact are the roots of the Macintosh interface. However, I am not any kind of Macintosh programmer, and I use *ResEdit* all the time. I used it to change my Trash can, edit my menus, change my watch cursor, and a variety of other tasks. I know of lots of people who, like myself, used *ResEdit* to "tweak" their programs in subtle ways. As a result, I decided to aim the book at non-programmers like myself. Programmers will want to buy it as well, because it still contains a lot of information about certain resources, but it will not tell you how to create your own TMPLs or about the internal workings of *ResEdit* itself. For that, I highly recommend Apple's own *ResEdit Reference Manual*, available from Addison-Wesley. It contains a lot more of the information programmers use. In addition, those of you who are somewhere between developers and intermediate users of *ResEdit* might want to take a look at Peter Alley's *ResEdit Complete*, also from Addison-Wesley, to see if it more to your liking.

Each article covers four general areas: an introduction, how to use the resource editor in question, technical information (where applicable), and a final section with tips and additional "exercises" you may wish to try. If you already know about what a resource does, skip ahead to the section dealing with the editor itself. Or, you may wish to go to the end of the article for new ideas about using this resource. After each article, there is a quick review of the major techniques discussed.

Some of you may be wondering about the title of this book. It is based on the title of the book *Zen and the Art of Motorcycle Maintenance*, which has become almost a shibboleth in the English language. The word *Zen* evokes images of mystical objects and people. A Zennist might be expected to talk about gateways into other planes of existence and powerful amulets. In short, Zen represents the mysterious and the bizarre. However, the philosophies of Zen, like many other philosophies and religions, also try to break very confusing concepts and thoughts into individual Truths. To a Zen practitioner, there are certain fundamental Truths which rule the Universe and all things in it.

Both of these definitions of Zen apply to the subject of this book. *ResEdit* has always been something of a mystical conundrum to the uninitiated. It may seem to occupy a different plane of existence, one that requires a deeper understanding of how a Macintosh works. As with Zen philosophy, one might hear a variety of ideas about the truths of *ResEdit*; some of these might be correct, but incorrect as well. This book, however, emphasizes the second definition of Zen. We have tried to break down *ResEdit* into simple truths which can be applied to many other situations in the computer world. We hope this book will give you the confidence to experiment with other resources as well. Yes, *ResEdit* can destroy your System and many other things. However, if one is careful and follows certain rules, it is possible to become something of a *ResEdit* guru. And, having attained such enlightenment, you'll want to share this experience with others. This is indeed the BMUG way.

Chapter One

What Are Resources?

by Brendan McCarthy

> *How Zennists carry on*
> *About the resources!*
> *What madness makes me edit,*
> *At noon, The midnight beep?*

What are resources?

In 1984 when Apple first unveiled the Macintosh, computer users and software developers alike were attracted to the innovative elegance of its now familiar user interface. There is a great consistency in the way the Mac "looks and feels," regardless of what program you are using. Resources are part of the reason for this. They are a pervasive, hidden aspect of what makes a Mac a Mac. Most users never deal with them directly.

Resources are discreet aspects, or components of the images you see on your screen—what they look like, and how they are displayed. Think of resources as the ingredients in a fine recipe, most of which are essential, others of which are optional, and all of which can be fudged a little.

In order to make this user interface easier to modify, the designers of the Macintosh have provided the Mac with an ability to understand resources, which are small chunks of program code, each of which can be individually modified with *ResEdit*. System software is largely composed of resources, as are programs written for the Mac, which usually "borrow" system resources in order to generate their own interface. This is an important part of why the Macintosh "looks and feels" the same in any program.

Every element of the Macintosh interface which we have come to know and love is a resource. Menus, icons, cursors, keyboard layouts, and many other things are resources. Any file or program running on a Mac has the potential to contain resources, in a section of the file know as the "resource fork." There is a similar portion of the file called the "data fork" where the actual numerical and textual data (such as in a word processing document) lives. Within the resource fork, each resource has several identifying markers. These are the type of resource, the ID number of the resource, and sometimes the name of the resource.

Of course, since we are dealing with a computer, this data is really just a stream of incomprehensible numbers. In the early days of Macintosh, creating or changing a resource usually involved a calculator and a large amount of caffeine. Thankfully, some engineers at Apple decided to use their calculators and caffeine-saturated carbonated beverages to make creating and editing resources less of a chore. When they were done a new age dawned, birds sang, flowers bloomed, and *ResEdit 1.0* was born. *ResEdit* is short for "Resource Editor," and it allows you to, as its name implies, edit some of these common resources graphically. The original *ResEdit* was very dangerous, and did very little to help the average user. New versions continued to come out, each with significant improvements. Later, as *System 7* became more and more of a reality, Apple realized that they were going to need a new *ResEdit* which could handle all the new resources in *System 7*. The most current result of that is *ResEdit 2.1.1*.

The Get Resource Info... dialog box: the beginner's view

When a program needs a resource (for instance, when the *Finder* puts a menu in the menu bar), the resource is not created on the spot. This would take a lot of time, and seriously affect the performance of a Macintosh, since the Mac is very resource-oriented. We all know that the Mac moves pretty quickly when it wants to, so the Mac uses stored resources to enhance speed.

What really happens, then, is that the program realizes that it needs to put Menu #5 into the menu bar, so it looks at its resource fork and pulls out Menu #5. It doesn't look at the menu to see if it says what it should; it just grabs all the info and throws it into the menu bar.

So if you've written something else and called it Menu #5, the program won't care. It will just toss your creation onto the menu bar. So how do you replace Menu # 5 with something else? Like most Macintosh applications, *ResEdit* lets you copy and paste, but *ResEdit* copies whole resources. Once you've pasted something into a file, you still need to call it by a name that the program recognizes. This is where the Get Resource Info... dialog box comes in to play. To get to it, go to the Resource menu and select the Get Resource Info... item.

```
▣□══════ Info for MENU 5 from Finder ══════◳

Type:    MENU              Size:   116
ID:     [5            ]
Name:   [                              ]
                              Owner type
    Owner ID: [            ]   DRVR  ⬆
                              WDEF  ▓
    Sub ID:   [            ]   MDEF  ⬇

Attributes:
  ☐ System Heap   ☐ Locked      ☒ Preload
  ☐ Purgeable     ☐ Protected   ☐ Compressed
```

Figure 1 -
The Get Resource Info...
dialog box.

This dialog box allows you to change the ID number and name of the resource. Very rarely does a program call a resource by its name, so this field is usually blank. If you wish to change the ID of a resource which you have pasted in or created within a program, click once on the particular resource (for instance, MENU ID 5 in a copy of the Finder), and choose Get Resource Info... from the Resource menu. You will see something very similar to Figure 1, above. If you're a beginner, you're only interested in the name and the ID number. If you wish to learn more about the check boxes below these two fields, see the next section. However, never change these check boxes unless you absolutely have to, and you know exactly what you're doing! Chaging these boxes can cause evil system errors.

If you don't know what you're doing with these, just leave them the way they are.

When changing the ID number of a resource, it is often very comforting to know that *ResEdit* will take good care of you while you're doing this. It will not allow you to change the resource number into something which already exists. You have to first delete or change the ID number of the resource you are replacing, and then change the ID number of the new resource. This may seem like a slow way to do things, but a slip of the fingers when typing in a new resource number could be disastrous if *ResEdit* allowed you to directly replace a resource.

Even if you are pasting a new resource into a file from an external source, and this resource has the same ID number as a resource of the same type which is already there, *ResEdit* will ask you if you want to replace the original resource with the new one, abort the whole operation (the default choice), or assign unique ID numbers to the new resources. This prevents you from doing anything accidental and ugly!

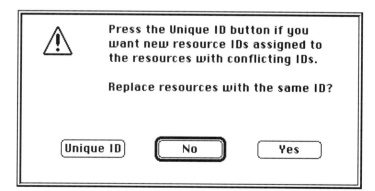

Figure 2 -
The replace same resource ID dialog box.

The *Get Resource Info...* dialog box for the more advanced user

In addition to the name and ID number of a resource, the Get Resource Info... dialog box allows you to change

Attributes	If Checked:	If Unchecked:
System Heap	When loaded into memory, the resource is placed in the system heap.	When loaded into memory, the resource is placed in the application heap.
Purgeable	When loaded, the resource may be unloaded if memory gets low.	When loaded, the resource will not be unloaded if memory gets low.
Locked	When loaded, the resource will not move around in memory.	When loaded, the resource may shift in memory to open up free space.
Protected	When unloaded, changes to the resource won't be written back to the resource file.	When unloaded, changes to the resource will be written back to the resource file.
Preload	Automatically loads the resource when its resource file is opened (on launch if it is in an application).	Doesn't load the resource until it is requested.
Compressed (System 7 only)	System compresses resource.	System does not compress resource.

Figure 3 -
Resource attributes.

various other attributes of the resource, which are represented by the check boxes at the bottom of the dialog box. As was said before, it is very important that you know what you're doing before you alter these. If a program expects to find a resource and you have set the "Purgeable" box to true, the program will probably not respond well when it finds out that the resource has been purged out of memory. The only people who usually need to know about these boxes are those who are writing their own programs. Some people may have problems with a resource which can be fixed by altering these boxes, but this is a rare case. However, if you are interested in these check boxes, Figure 2, left, outlines the function of each one.

As I have said, changing these attributes can cause many problems. However, there are a few common problems which you can avoid. For instance, making a resource available to the System Heap will make it available to all running applications, but may cause problems if the System Heap is already crowded. If you make a resource purgeable, memory will be freed up if needed, but this will no doubt confuse the application looking for a resource which has disappeared. One of the resources which will inevitably cause problems if it has disappeared is the MENU resource. Marking a resource "Locked" may cause memory to fragment (making it harder for applications to get the amount they request), but an application that assumes a resource will be locked may crash and burn if an unlocked resource unexpectedly shifts in memory. Marking a resource "Preload" may slow down the launch of an application, but the resource will be in memory the instant it's needed. On the other hand, unnecessarily preloading a resource may take up valuable memory.

Before you begin adding resources helter-skelter, you should realize that there is a restriction on which ID numbers may be used for a resource. Numbers which fall between -32768 and 127 are reserved for the six-colored god, Apple Computer. Everything between 128 and 32767 may be used by everyone else.

Playing it safe

If you keep the following rules in mind, playing with *ResEdit* will be more like a tiptoe through the tulips than a muddle through the minefield. These should become mantras to you as you go through this book.

- Always work on a backup file. Always have a backup of your disk. Never work on the original file. What would you do if you caused a fatal error? Read this again until you understand it!

- Don't change the "Owner ID" and "Sub ID" attributes of a resource unless you really know what you're doing.

- Never remove a resource unless you're absolutely sure it's not used. Missing resources can wreak havoc with an application.

- Never distribute an altered version of an application to anyone else. Users may get confused when things don't look and act as they expect.

As you can see, playing with resource attributes can be like playing with fire; you might burn down the forest, or you might create something fun and interesting.

Manipulating resources with *ResEdit*

This section will talk about some of the ways in which resources can be manipulated with *ResEdit*. By the end of this article, you will already be able to do many interesting things with *ResEdit*. The real fun starts in the next chapters, however, when you'll learn how to actually edit the resources. Here are some concepts which you'll need to know first.

Creating a new resource: When you're in any window of *ResEdit*, except for the editors themselves, you can choose Create New Resource... from the Resource menu. If you are in the main window of *ResEdit* (the window which shows all the resources in the resource fork), this command will bring up a dialog box which will let you type in the type of resource you wish to create. If you have already opened one of the resource types (by double-clicking on its icon in the main window) and are looking at a list of, for instance, all the MENU resources, this command will create a new resource of that type, assigning it a unique ID number.

Duplicating a resource: One way to make a backup is to duplicate the original resource. Then you can edit the original, and you will still have a safe copy, contained within the file itself. The command for this is Duplicate, and it is found in the Edit menu.

Clipboard actions: As stated earlier, *ResEdit* allows you to copy, cut and paste resources to and from the Clipboard (in reality, *ResEdit* uses its own special Clipboard which is capable of handling the resources as simple objects rather than code). Simply choose a resource (you can select all the resources of a single type by clicking once on the appropriate icon in the main window) and choose the desired action from the Edit menu. With these commands, you can create files of all your favorite resources (such as icons) and copy and paste them wherever you want.

Selecting multiple resources: individual resources or resource types may be selected as a group. To select two consecutive resources, hold down the Shift key when you select them. To select non-consecutive resources, use the Command key. If you use the Shift key to select two non-consecutive resources, *ResEdit* will select all the resources between those two resources. This can either be very time-saving or very frustrating, if you do it unintentionally.

Practice makes perfect

If you wish to experiment with all these concepts, go right ahead. Make a backup copy of the disk which came with the book, open up *ResEdit 2.1* (which is on the disk in a self-extracting archive, so you'll have to move the archive to another disk to uncompress it), and play with some of the files on this disk. If you've made a backup (or locked the disk), you won't do any permanent damage, so you can try all of these things.

Happy ResEditing!

Resources overview

To access the *Get Resource Info…* dialog box

- Open *ResEdit*
- Open the program you wish to look at or alter
- Open up the type of resource you wish to look at (e.g., ICON)
- Click once on the specific resource you want to look at (e.g., ICON #128)
- Select Get Resource Info… from the Resource menu

To duplicate a resource:

- Select the specific resource you wish to duplicate (e.g., ICON #128)
- Choose Duplicate from the Edit menu

To create a blank resource of a certain type:

- Open up the type of resource you wish to add to (e.g., ICON)
- Choose Create New Resource… from the Resource menu

To create a new type of resource:

- Open (with *ResEdit*) the file you want to add to
- Choose Create New Resource… in the main window of the file
- Type (or select from the list) the type of resource you wish to add

Brendan McCarthy has been wrestling with the Macintosh Toolbox since 1985. Brendan is currently employed as a software engineer at Claris Corporation, where he has collaborated on MacProject II 2.0 and FileMaker Pro. Brendan has also been sighted prowling in lightless caverns, steamy rain forests, Irish moors, and gloomy nightclubs.

Chapter Two

Moving Resources

by Derrick Schneider

*Fallen leaves –
moving,
yet not moving.*

Moving resources

In addition to being a resource editor, *ResEdit* can function as a resource mover. By simply cutting, copying, and pasting, you can quickly move resources from one place to another. This can be extremely useful if you are designing your own *HyperCard* stacks or *MicroPhone II* scripts. Rather than limit yourself to the resources they provide, why not add ones which you think are better? Despite the fact that the concept of this is simple enough, it can still get kind of tricky determining exactly where to insert a resource. This section will explain the concept of hierarchy, so that you as the reader will know where to put the resources that we're going to show you how to create and edit in later chapters.

Hierarchy: The resource tree

So what is hierarchy? In the context we're using, it means where the Macintosh looks for resources. Basically, when a program needs a resource for some purpose, it follows a particular sequence in its quest for that resource. There are two ways of visualizing that sequence. One is that the Mac looks in the most recently opened file first. So let's say you're working on a *HyperCard* script, and you decide to associate a button with the script and an icon with that button. You tell this to *HyperCard* and it provides you with a list of icons. But how does this work? First *HyperCard* itself intercepts the call that the icon list is needed. Then it looks at the most recently opened file—your stack—and tacks all the icons in that stack into the icon list. Then it looks at the next most recently opened file—*HyperCard* itself—and finds all the icon resources there, and adds them to the list. Finally, *HyperCard* looks at the file which was opened first—the System file, which is always open once you get a "Happy Mac" at startup. For a visual representation of this, see Figure 1, next page.

Bedford Claims
Office
685 - 3750

9AM TUES @ FIN PRYSCO INT

CALL FIRST ON MONDAY FOR TUES APPMT

AAA - CHANGES TO AD

LEVY — CHANGES TO AD & B/C IDEAS

GALLAGHER — CHANGES TO AD

DALLAS
13342 FLOYD CIRCLE

669-0951

METRO **214-263-3199**
WATS **1-800-442-4192**
FAX **214-235-7317**

ARLINGTON-FT. WORTH
2227 E. DIVISION

METRO **817-640-0505**

WATS **1-800-552-7797**
FAX **817-640-0512**

AUTO GLASS • RESIDENTIAL & PLATE GLASS • T-TOPS • WHEEL COVERS • TINTING

Figure 1 –

One way to look at the hierarchy structure. Here, a program tries to get its resources from the most recently opened file first.

There is a different way to look at this which is perhaps better for understanding where these resources come from. It goes along these lines: a document may get resources from itself, the application it belongs to, and the System file; an application may get resources from itself and the System file; and the System file can only get resources from itself. Figure 2, below, explains this a little bit better. Thus, a document, such as a *HyperCard* stack, will be able to access resources from all of these places. When *HyperCard* calls for the icons then, it gathers up all the resources available and presents the familiar icon selection box.

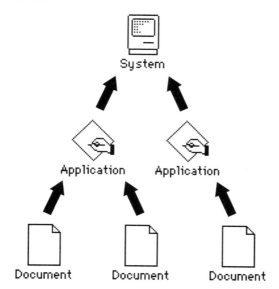

Figure 2 –

The other way to look at hierarchical structure. Here, files at the bottom of the tree have access to all the resources up the line, and levels which are higher up do not have access to the resources below them.

If one of these makes more sense to you than the other, by all means use that one. These are just two ways of visualizing where resources come from and how they get there. The end result is the same.

So now let's apply these to some real examples. Let's say you're a budding *HyperCard* scripter and you want to use a custom icon in one of your stacks. Where should you put it? Common sense might tell you to throw the thing into the stack itself. But will you want to use this icon in other stacks? In that case, it will be less of a hassle if you put the icon into *HyperCard* itself. That way, anytime you want to use that icon, no matter what stack you're in, the icon will be there; you won't have to re-paste it into each and every stack. But wait, there's more! Are you going to distribute this stack in any way? If so, what will happen when another person, using their own copy of *HyperCard*, looks at that button? Since the icon that the button looks for is stowed away in your copy of *HyperCard*, the same script running under a different *HyperCard* won't be able to find the icon, and you won't be able to show off your amazing ability to make your own cool icons. In fact, *HyperCard* will simply not show the icon for that button. But if the icon is in the stack, then, when the stack draws the button, it will find the icon which is associated with it, and you will look pretty amazing.

Let's look at one more example. Let's say you've got a great sound that you want to use in your *HyperCard* stack, in a *MicroPhone II* script, and as your System beep. Where do you put it? The System itself. That way, it will be available globally to anything which has the capacity to use it.

As you can see, working with hierarchy does not have a set formula. You must decide where to place your resources according to how they'll be used. Using the information in the above section, however, should give you the capability to figure out where something should go. Just remember, every time you move a resource into a file, that file gets bigger, either in physical size, RAM size, or both.

Common resources to move around

As I said before, *ResEdit* can also function as a resource mover. Even resources which don't have any editors to speak of are worked with constantly under *ResEdit*.

If you look at snd resources, FKEYs, or XCMDs with *ResEdit*, you'll be faced with a horrible display of hexadecimal representation of code. However, you should not be discouraged by this. These resources can add quite a lot to your life. FKEYs can be used to enhance the abilities of your Macintosh with a quick keystroke. Sounds can add a new life to your programs, stacks, and scripts, as well as alerting you if need be. XCMDs extend the capabilities of *MicroPhone II*, *HyperCard*, and many other programs from within scripts themselves. Just because they look ugly doesn't mean you shouldn't deal with them. You can, of course, copy and paste them from their sources for your own purposes. But some of these common resources can also be modified with *ResEdit*. Let's take a look at some of them.

FKEYs

FKEYs (which is the resource name as well as the common name) add quite a lot to your Macintosh. They are small programs which can be accessed from your keyboard in a wide variety of situations (if they're in the System file; otherwise, they are only available from the program where they are installed). Many people are familiar with the built-in FKEYs which come with every Mac. By holding down Command, Shift, and the number 3, you can take a picture of your screen in *MacPaint* (or PICT format in System 7) which can be opened by just about any graphics program. By typing Command-Shift-4, you can force your printer to print a picture of the screen. Command-Shift-1 will eject a disk from your internal drive, while Command-Shift-2 ejects the disk from your second floppy drive. So how do you work with these?

Using these FKEYs can be kind of tricky. Under System 6, the Screen Shot FKEY (Command-Shift-3) works only in black and white, has trouble with some larger monitors, and saves the screen in MacPaint format. Under System 7, it works under all conditions, saving its document as a PICT file that can be opened in TeachText. The Print Screen FKEY (Command-Shift-4) works only on ImageWriter printers. If you have any other printer, take a screen shot, open it in your graphics program and print from there.

If you've downloaded an FKEY from a bulletin board, or gotten one from a friend, open the FKEY file with *ResEdit*. Copy the resource (this way you'll still have a copy of the original) and paste it into a copy of the System. Make a note of the ID number. Move your new System into the System Folder and reboot the computer. Do you still remember the ID number? That is the number you type, with Command and Shift held down, to activate the FKEY. Thus, if your new FKEY has an ID number of 5, typing Command-Shift-5 will call it up.

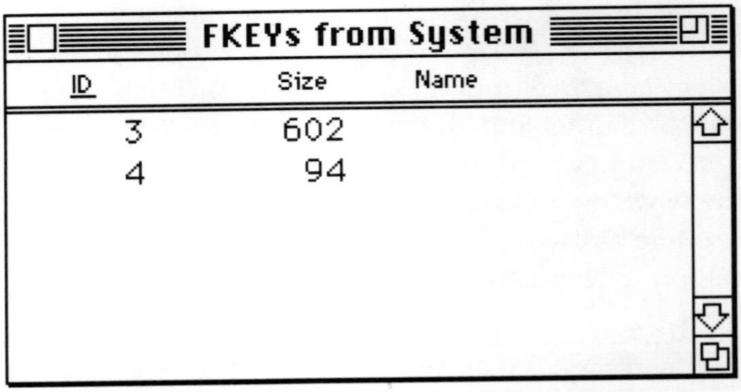

☐	FKEYs from System		⌐
ID	Size	Name	
3	602		
4	94		

Figure 3 –

The FKEY picker window in *ResEdit*.

Sooner or later, as you install more and more FKEYs, you're going to have two FKEYs which have the same ID number. Inevitably, they will be the two FKEYs you really want in your System. Don't worry, though. The problem can be fixed.

Just remember that the ID number of the FKEY determines the key used to activate it. When the programmer makes an FKEY, he or she doesn't somehow code into the FKEY which number should be activating it. All you have to do to have both FKEYs is to change the ID numbers. Make sure that both ID numbers are between 0 and 9, and you're all set! You'll now have both FKEYs available to you.

The snd resource

One of the greatest advantages of a Macintosh is the ability to play pre-recorded sounds. This is familiar to most of us, even if it is only the beep sound which your computer uses to get your attention. Perhaps you've been using a *HyperCard* stack and discovered a cool sound which pops up when you push a button. These are all examples of snd resources. (Note: In reality, the snd resource has an extra space after it, making it the 'snd ' resource. For aesthetic purposes, this space has been omitted from this article.)

If you've gotten ahold of a sound resource you wish to install as a beep or into a *HyperCard* stack or a *MicroPhone II* script, you can copy and paste it with *ResEdit*. But what if you've opened up a program with *ResEdit* and you see it has snd resources? You might not know what they sound like, or whether you'd want to use one as a beep sound. Fortunately, *ResEdit* has an option to let you listen to them.

≡≡≡ snds from System ≡≡≡		
ID	Size	Name
1	228	"Simple Beep"
2	11206	"Clink-Klank"
3	7829	"Boing"
4	2208	"Monkey"

Figure 4 –
The snd picker window in *ResEdit.*

If you have the list of all the snd resources open in front of you (accessed by double-clicking on the snd icon in *ResEdit's* main window), click once on a sound (clicking twice is not recommended for the faint of heart, since it produces an incredibly complex display of assembly language, but you're more than welcome to take a look), and choose Try Sound from the snd menu. For a fun effect, you can try playing an octave in the middle C range with the sound by choosing Try Scale With Sound.

There's a lot of technical information about sounds which you can read if you're interested, but it's not essential for understanding how to move them about. In general, sound resources are stored in two formats, called "format 1 snd" and "format 2 snd." Format 1 snd resources can contain either sampled sound (made with the *MacRecorder*, for instance) or wave table data. This wave table data specifies a melody by a sequence of commands but doesn't specify an actual sound. Think of this as sheet music that only has the notes but doesn't say that you must play it on a guitar. Format 2 snd was developed for use with *HyperCard*. By using the Try as HyperCard Sound command in the snd menu, you can hear what the sound will sound like in *HyperCard*. This format is intended to be used with sampled sound only, not wave table data. This is a major cause of confusion for many users. However, it should be noted that *HyperCard 2.x* is capable of playing both format 1 sounds and format 2 sounds.

When using these resources to hold sampled sound data, the data can be sampled at rates up to 22KHz. This means that in theory the sound can contain harmonics up to 1/2 the sampling rate (or 11KHz). This is known as the Nyquist frequency. In actuality, the sampling rate must be 2.5 times the highest frequency you want to sample, but for practical purposes the .5 is rounded down.

Sometimes this can cause a problem when playing samples on the Macintosh. I'm sure you all have experienced a sound that sounds like the Munchkins, even though it's supposed to be John Cleese. Or how about the sound that you could swear is Lurch, even though it's supposed to be Captain Kirk! By changing the sampling rate of these sounds (actually the playback rate) you can fix this problem.

Though *ResEdit* doesn't provide easy editing of this, many shareware utilities do. When using any program that allows you to renumber or rename snd resources, you should keep in mind that numbers 0 through 8191 are reserved by Apple. This means that if you use these numbers for your sound and then someday your sound (or application) doesn't work, you can't sue Apple!

One major problem with sounds is the amount of memory they take up. Large or complex sounds can take up a lot of RAM and a lot of physical space in the program. Keep this in mind if you are a sound-o-phile.

If you are really interested in working with sounds, you'll want to check out Chris Reed's snd editor, included on the disk with the book. Follow the instructions in the text file that goes with the editor, and you'll be set with a really cool snd editor, capable of quite a lot functionality. For more information about installing editors, read "Installing Editors." Figure 5 shows a sound opened with this editor.

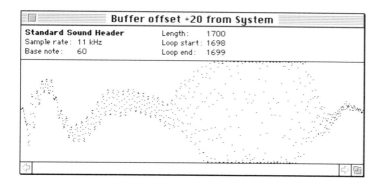

Figure 5 –
The snd editor.

Under *System 7*, there are some significant changes in the way in which sounds are moved around. For instance, the Scrapbook and Clipboard are capable of holding snd resources, and even playing them. Also, sounds may be dragged directly into the System file, which can be opened and viewed for operations such as this. As an alternate way to paste a sound into your System, copy the snd resource (sorry, it has to be in this format for now), open the Sound Control Panel, and choose Paste from the Edit menu. The System will ask you to name the sound, and then it will install the snd resource directly into the System file for you.

XCMDs

For those of you who are *HyperCard* scriptors, you've probably come across XCMDs and their near relatives, XFCNs. These stand for "eXternal CoMmanD" and "eXternal FunCtioN," respectively. Like FKEYs, XCMDs and XFCNs are called by the names of the resources they contain. Most stacks which contain special XCMDs or XFCNs (usually grouped under the one name, XCMD) offer an option to install the XCMD directly into the stack of your choice. However, this is not necessarily the case (though *HyperCard* scriptors who do not should get a slap on the wrist for this lack of interface), and you can use *ResEdit* if that's true. In addition to getting new XCMDs, you may wish to move one which you use frequently out of a stack or similar document. You really can't do anything like preview them or modify the calls to them as you can with snds and FKEYs. Still, it's a common resource that gets moved around, so I figured I should mention it and shed some light on it.

With this information, you will be able to decide where to put resources, and you now know how to work with some common resources which don't have editors.

Moving resources overview

To make a resource available to only one document:

- Paste the resource directly into that document

While not editing books or hanging out with the BMUG gang, Derrick Schneider is a junior/senior (depending on when you read this) at UC Berkeley, where all great things originate. Despite a strong interest in computers, Derrick is actually a zoology major, intending to go into veterinary medicine. He is determined to conquer the dreaded "BMUG syndrome" which tends to prevent Berkeley students from graduating while involved with the user group. He can be reached at DFS BMUG on America Online and UG0127, the BMUG account on AppleLink.

Thanks to Joe Zobkiw for his information about sound resources. He can be reached at AFL Zobkiw an America Online.

To make a resource available to any document made with an application:

- Paste the resource into the application

To make a resource available to any application, including the System:

- Paste the resource into the System file

To change the activation key of an FKEY:

- Open *ResEdit*, and use it to open the file which contains the FKEY
- Select the FKEY you wish to modify, and choose Get Resource Info…
- Change the ID number to any key between 0 and 9. This number, plus Command and Shift, will activate the FKEY

To listen to a sound:

- Open *ResEdit*, and use it to open the file which contains the sound. Click twice on the snd icon in *ResEdit*
- Click once on the sound you wish to hear, and then choose Try Sound from the snd menu

Chapter Three

Customizing Your Finder

by Tom Chavez

Magnificent! Magnificent!
No one knows the final word.
The Finder's layout aflame,
Out of the void leap wooden windows.

Customizing your Finder

One of the more fun uses for *ResEdit* is to customize the visual aspects of the Finder. Much of what I am covering here can be accomplished with the public domain tool called *Layout* (also included with the commercial *Norton Utilities* package). However, if you were wondering how it all works, here is a good description.

First things first. Launch *ResEdit* and open a copy of the Finder file. This should be on another disk, so that the Mac does not become confused about which Finder to use. Once you have finished making the changes, simply move your old Finder out of the System Folder and replace it with the file you have made the changes to.

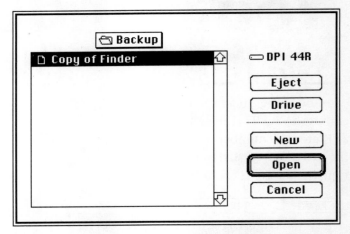

Figure 1 –

Opening copy of Finder.

The Finder used for the screens shown in this article was version 6.0.7, but the layout information has not changed during the 6.0.x series of System software. However, if you are using System 7, most of this article is useless. Skip to the end and read about the Views Control Panel. System 7 no longer stores its Finder information in the LAYO resource. Now the system uses the information in the fval resource, but many attempts to fiddle with this have been unsuccessful. If you want to poke around with this resource, there is one in the Finder and one in the Finder Preferences.

The resource type that we are going to be editing is the LAYO resource. This is short for LAYOut, and it controls the way things are set up in the Finder. Go ahead and open it by double-clicking on the LAYO icon.

If your copy of the Finder is like mine, you should have only one LAYO resource, whose ID is 128. The size is fixed at 66 bytes. Fewer than that would not be enough room for the Finder to have all the necessary information. More than that would have extra (useless) information at the end of the record.

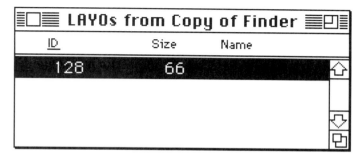

Figure 2 –
The LAYO Picker.

One thing you may wish to do is to duplicate the current LAYO ID=128 resource, edit it as a resource with a different ID number, and then switch the ID numbers of the two resources so that your changes take effect the next time the Finder is run, such as after a reboot.

Figure 3 –
The LAYO editor.

25

Opening specific resources (such as LAYO ID=128) can be accomplished by double-clicking on the resource, selecting the resource and hitting <Return>, or typing in the name of the resource and hitting <Return>. You only need to type as many letters as needed so that *ResEdit* knows which one to open. For instance, typing 'L' would select the LAYO resource, since that is the only one which begins with an L.

Customizing

For clarity's sake, I have broken down the four windows of data which make up the LAYO resource and grouped them roughly by similar function, showing them a few at a time. Therefore, you can skip those fields you already understand, and learn about those which are new to you.

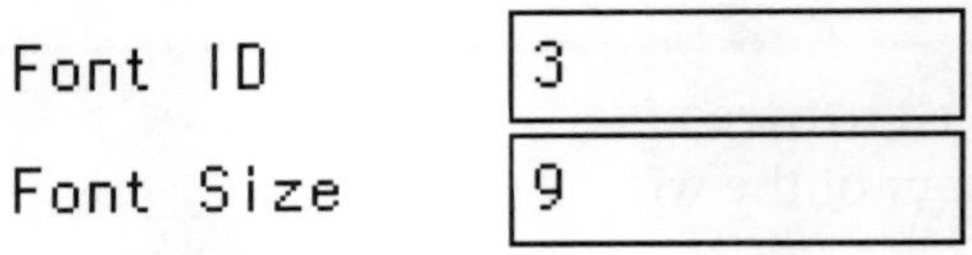

Figure 4 –
The font ID and size fields in the LAYO editor.

```
Font ID      [ 3 ]
Font Size    [ 9 ]
```

Font ID is the font family number used for displaying text in a window (filenames, dates, etc.). The default is 3 (Geneva). I prefer 33 (Avant Garde). The **Font Size** is the size (in points) of the text in all windows—icon view, and small icon view to all of the text views (such as View by Name and View by Date.)

Screen Header Height sets how far down in the content area of the window (the actual window, not including the title bar at the top) the vertical scroll bar and icons start. The default is 20, which allows space for the extra information the Finder puts at the top of every window.

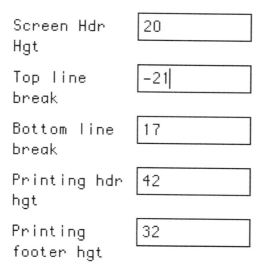

Screen Hdr Hgt `20`

Top line break `-21|`

Bottom line break `17`

Printing hdr hgt `42`

Printing footer hgt `32`

Figure 5 –
Text view header fields.

Top line break determines where the first line of text will appear in text views. Don't change this from the default value of -21.

Bottom line break value determines how much space is left between the last line of text in a text view and the bottom of the window.

The **printing height** fields set the header and footer sizes for printed pages.

Window Rect `62` `14` `250` `418` `Set`

Figure 6 –
Window default size fields.

Window Rect is the default size of the window used whenever a new folder is created. Of course the window can be resized after you create it; these values just determine the initial size. The fields represent the size and the location of the window, with the first two fields showing the coordinates of the top left corner, and the last two fields showing the coordinates of the bottom right corner of the window. If you are confused about these numbers, just keep in mind that the upper left corner of the screen is 0,0 and that Macintoshes usually have 72 dots per inch on their screen. So, if the first field is 62 and the second field is 14, the left corner of new windows will appear 62 pixels (.86 inches) from the top of the screen and 14 pixels (.19 inches) from the left edge.

The **Set** button can be used to make a rectangle without knowing the actual values. When you click on the Set button, *ResEdit* expects you to click and drag a rectangle, and that rectangle becomes the Window Rect. One caution: if you click outside of a *ResEdit* window while running MultiFinder, you will be switched out of *ResEdit*, and the rectangle will not be set.

Line spacing	16
Tab stop 1	20
Tab stop 2	144
Tab stop 3	184
Tab stop 4	280
Tab stop 5	376
Tab stop 6	424
Tab stop 7	456
Column Justification	$02

Figure 7 –

Tab position fields for the Finder's list view.

Line spacing is the point spacing from one line to the next. The default is 16 points, or pixels. You can increase it for more space between lines in the text views, or decrease it to show more filenames at one time.

```
╒═□═════════════ ResEdit 2.1 ═══════════════□═╕
│  Name              Size  Kind          Last Modified       │
│ ┌─────────────────────────────────────────────┐
│ │ 🗋 Cursors          1K  ResEdit document  Sun, Mar 3, 1991   3:│⬆
│ │ 🗋 Icons            1K  ResEdit document  Sun, Mar 3, 1991   3:│
│ │ ◈ ResEdit        622K  application       Thu, Dec 6, 1990   12│
│ │                                                │
│ │                                                │⬇
│ ◁│                                               │▷▫│
```

Figure 8 –

An example of a Finder window showing a list view.

The **Tab Stops** determine how much space is allotted for the columns which show name, size, kind, etc. Tab stop 1 indicates that the name will start 20 pixels from the left edge of the window. Tab stop 2 is for the size; Tab 3 is for kind; Tab 4 is the last modified date; Tab 5 is the last modified time; Tab 6 is for the lock icon (shown when a file is locked via the Get Info dialog); Tab 7 marks the end of the space for the lock icon. The Get Info... dialog mentioned here is the one which you can access from the File menu in the Finder. Do not confuse this with the Get Resource Info... dialog box available in *ResEdit*.

When a field is justified to the right (rather than the default, left), the text will be justified to the next tab stop, rather than starting from the listed tab. For example, when left justified, the name will start at pixel 20; when right justified, the name will end at pixel 143.

To set the justification, enter a number in the column justification field. Compute this value with the following formula:

Start with 0 (all left justified)

Add 1 ($01) to right justify the Name field

Add 2 ($02) to right justify the Size field

Add 4 ($04) to right justify the Kind field

Add 8 ($08) to right justify the Last Modified date field

Add 16 ($10) to right justify the Last Modified time field

Add 32 ($20) to right justify the Lock field.

As shown above, the justification is set to right justify the Size field. This makes the sizes line up in a nice column

29

with the "K"s all in a line, rather than lining up the first digits in a column.

I digress here for a quick lesson about hexadecimal. In *ResEdit*, a "$" preceding a number indicates that it is in hexadecimal, or base 16. Base 16 counts a bit differently than regular decimal:

0 = $0	8 = $8	16 = $10	24 = $18
1 = $1	9 = $9	17 = $11	25 = $19
2 = $2	10 = $A	18 = $12	26 = $1A
3 = $3	11 = $B	19 = $13	27 = $1B
4 = $4	12 = $C	20 = $14	28 = $1C
5 = $5	13 = $D	21 = $15	29 = $1D
6 = $6	14 = $E	22 = $16	30 = $1E
7 = $7	15 = $F	23 = $17	31 = $1F

As you can see, hexadecimal doesn't become two digits (carry over) until sixteen is reached, at which point it carries a one to the next higher digit, just like base 10. At the next multiple of sixteen, it carries over again to become $20.

If this doesn't make much sense to you, that's probably because you were born with ten fingers rather than sixteen. *ResEdit* will let you use decimal values instead of hexadecimal. Just enter the appropriate decimal value, and make sure that you do not include the dollar sign.

Figure 9 –
U Don't Touch This.

Reserved $00

Bad karma can come from editing reserved fields. Not only that, it can cause serious problems with your Desktop file!

The next three fields all control the layout of icons in the View by Icon mode.

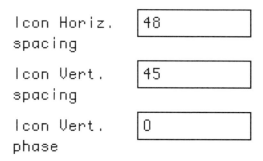

Figure 10 –
Icon spacing fields.

Icon Horizontal spacing sets the amount of pixels between icons horizontally. The default for this is 64; as you can see, I space my icons a bit closer together.

Icon Vertical spacing sets the pixel spacing between the icons vertically. The default for this is also 64, but 45 is enough to place one row of icons just below the text (names) of the row above.

Icon Vertical Phase determines whether the icons appear in a straight row, or if they are staggered up and down, with every other icon at a different vertical offset. This can be useful for long filenames that tend to run into each other. Just set the Vertical Phase to something like 31, and the names will not run into each other.

```
Sm. Icon     96
Horiz.

Sm. Icon     20
Vert.
```

Figure 11 –
Small icon space fields.

The two fields which control small icons are exactly like the fields which control large icons. **Small Icon Horizontal** controls the horizontal spacing of icons in the small icon view, while **Small Icon Vertical** controls the vertical spacing.

31

Figure 12 –
The new window default
view field.

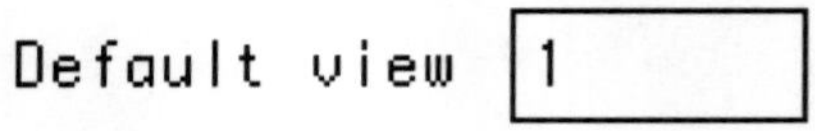

Default view [1]

Default view is the window type that will be used
when new windows are created. The choices are:

0	small icon view
1	icon view
2	by name
3	by date
4	by size
5	by kind

Figure 13 –
The text view date field.

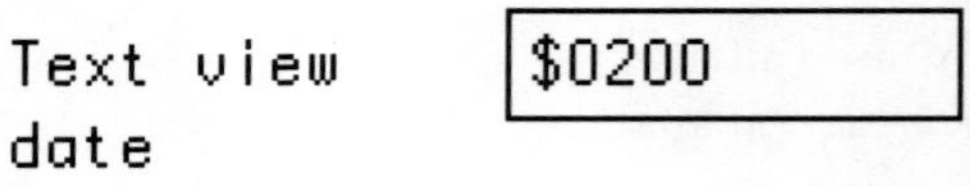

Text view
date [$0200]

Text view date controls how the date is shown in any
of the text views. There are three formats for the date field:

$0000 short date   e.g., 10/3/90
$0100 long date   e.g., Wednesday, October 3, 1990
$0200 abbreviated   e.g., Wed, Oct 3, 1990

The following are a set of true/false (yes/no) choices
for certain features of the Finder. In these choices, 0 equals
false (or No), 1 equals true (or Yes).

Use zoom   ◉ 0   ○ 1
Rects

Skip trash   ○ 0   ◉ 1
warnings

Figure 14–
Built-in Finder feature
choices.

Always grid   ◉ 0   ○ 1
drags

32

Use Zoom Rects controls whether or not the fancy animated zooming rectangles will be used whenever you open or close a folder or disk, or open and close applications. I turn these off just because they take time to happen; I want my windows to open and close more quickly.

The **Skip Trash Warnings** choice lets you get rid of the safety dialogs "Are you sure you want to remove the application <name>?" and "Are you sure you want to remove the system file <name>?." You can also prevent this from happening by holding down the Option key when you throw away a file. This button just allows you to set the default. If you are prone to throw away things that you don't mean to, set this to false. **Always Grid Drags** turns on the icon locking which prevents a window from having icons cluttered all over each other. This forces an icon onto the grid set by the horizontal and vertical spacing. Setting this to true helps you stay neater. In fact, you won't be able to place an icon off of the grid (unless you hold down the Command key while dragging). This can cause a conflict with icon phase, since the grid has evenly spaced intervals. If you use icon phase (mentioned above), you will find that that value has to be 0 or 31, since the grid does not allow icons to be moved to values which are not on it.

Icon-text gap   `0`

Figure 15 –
The icon-text gap field.

Icon-text gap increases the distance between an icon and the name below it. If you want to put some space between your icons and their names, set this to a higher value.

Sort Style   `4`

Figure 16 –
The sort style field.

At the top of the text view windows, the name of the field by which the window was sorted is underlined. In the illustration, a "view by name" window, the word "Name" is underlined, showing that the sort took place with that field.

If you want a different style to be used for the text of the "view by" field, such as bold italic, enter a number based on this formula:

Start with 0 ($0) for plain text
Add 1 ($1) for **bold**
Add 2 ($2) for *italic*
Add 4 ($4) for <u>underline</u>
Add 8 ($8) for outline
Add 16 ($10) for shadow
Add 32 ($20) for compressed
Add 64 ($40) for expanded

So for bold italic, the magic number would be 3 (1 for bold + 2 for italic).

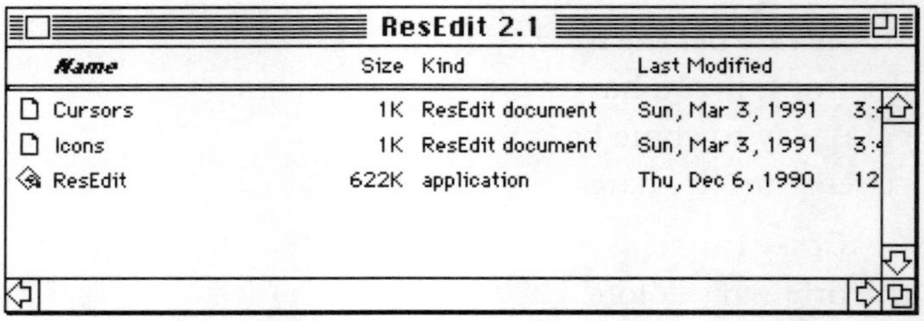

Figure 17 –

Example of window with sort style set at 3 (bold italic).

Name	Size	Kind	Last Modified	
☐ Cursors	1K	ResEdit document	Sun, Mar 3, 1991	3:4
☐ Icons	1K	ResEdit document	Sun, Mar 3, 1991	3:4
☒ ResEdit	622K	application	Thu, Dec 6, 1990	12

ResEdit 2.1

The **Watch Threshold** controls how quickly the cursor changes to a watch for time-consuming operations. The number is measured in ticks, which are 60ths of a second. As shown, the watch cursor will not appear until two seconds after a process starts. Thus, for tasks which take less than two seconds, you won't see the watch, and for longer tasks, it comes up after two seconds.

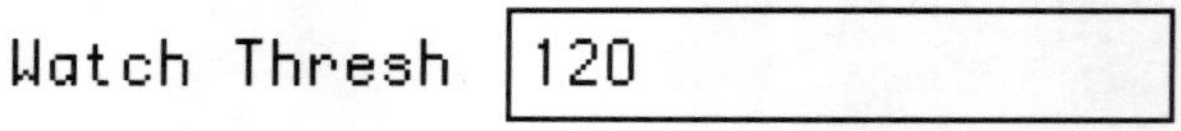

Figure 18 –

The watch threshold field.

Watch Thresh 120

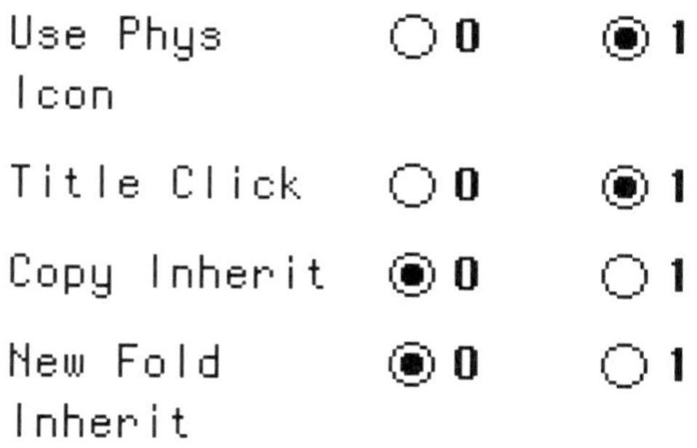

Use Phys   ○ 0   ⦿ 1
Icon

Title Click   ○ 0   ⦿ 1

Copy Inherit   ⦿ 0   ○ 1

New Fold   ⦿ 0   ○ 1
Inherit

Figure 19 –
More Finder feature choices.

Use Physical Icon replaces the standard disk, CD, and hard drive icons with pictures representing their physical locations. There are icons for the Mac Plus, SE, II, IIcx, Portable, etc. These icons help you see exactly which disk you are using.

Title Click lets you double-click in the Title bar of a window to open its parent window. For example, if you are looking at the System Folder on your hard disk, and your hard disk window is not showing, if you double-click on the title bar the hard disk window opens and comes to the front, if you have set the Title Click to true. This is a good way to come back out from a deep folder if you've covered up the parent windows.

Copy Inherit sets whether a copy of a folder inherits the original's colors, view-by setting, etc.

New Folder Inherit determines whether a new folder will have the same color, view-by setting, etc. of the parent folder.

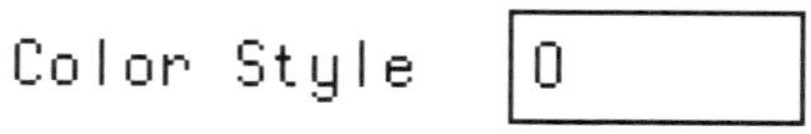

Color Style   [0]

Figure 20 –
Icon color style field.

Color Style determines how icons are filled in on color systems:

0 means that the black pixels are colored
1 means that the white pixels (interiors) are colored

For those with lots of screen real estate, the standard 13 open window maximum may not be enough. I have raised my maximum to 20 and find that if I open more windows than that, I cover up too much space on the screen.

Figure 21 –
Maximum number of Finder windows field.

```
Max # of          13
windows
```

If you've given the Finder the capability to open a larger number of windows, you may wish to increase the Finder's memory allotment in MultiFinder. To do this, click once on the Finder's icon in the System Folder, choose Get Info... from the File menu, and go to the field next to "Application memory size." Type in the new value you wish to allow the Finder (making sure it's no lower

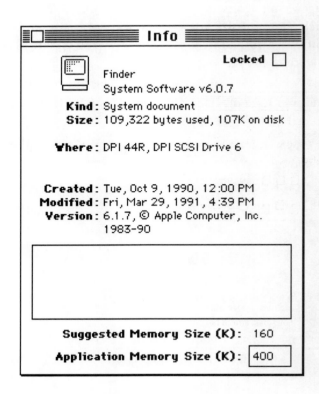

Figure 22 –
The Finder Get Info... box.

than 160). This is especially useful if you do a lot of copying of large files. On my 8-meg machine, the Finder's memory allocation is 400k (see Figure 22, previous page).

Well, we've reached the end of the LAYO resource. With the tips above, you can change the look of the *Finder* to suit your own needs. You might want to write down what you change, as it will not be maintained when you reinstall or upgrade your system software. Many times I've forgotten what I've changed, so I edit some parts, and then exit *ResEdit*, only to see that it just doesn't look the same. So now I have a list next to my Mac. Actually, this is a good idea for all the changes you might make with *ResEdit*.

If you are running under *System 7*, you will not find the LAYO resource in the Finder. Instead, you can make most of the changes described here with the Views Control Panel (See Figure 23, below). This will allow you to stagger your icons, make grid drags, and even choose which font and size you wish to use on the desktop, in addition to providing some new features which aren't covered by the LAYO resource.

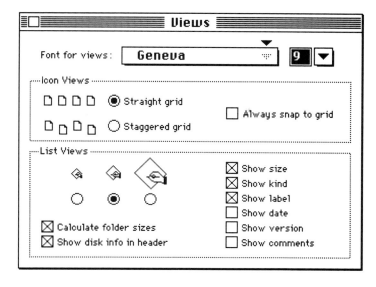

Figure 23 –

System 7's Views Control Panel.

Now you might have some time to further customize your Finder by changing cursors (in CURS), dialog and alert layout (in DLOG, ALRT, and DITL), icons (in ICN#), or menu text and command keys (in MENU). These are all covered in other sections of this book.

Have fun. And remember, **always edit a *copy* of your source file**. You'd hate to lose your only copy! And when you have something you like, make a backup copy.

LAYO overview

To get to the LAYO resource (System 6 only):

- Open *ResEdit*
- Open a copy of the *Finder*
- Double-click on the LAYO icon
- Double-click on LAYO ID#128

To change the font and font size in the Finder:

- Type the ID number of the font into the "Font ID" field
- Type the size of the font into the "Font Size" field

To stagger your icons

- Set "Icon Vert. Phase" to a number such as 31

To remove the trash warnings:

- Click on the "1" (true) button next to "Skip trash warnings"

To remove the animated zoom rectangles which appear when opening a file or folder:

- Click on the "0" button next to "Use zoom rects"

Tom Chavez is a Product Manager for Apple Computer, Inc. He was a co-founder of BMUG back when it was run by Tom, Raines, Reese, and a core team. Tom has worked at Apple for the past two and a half years since he graduated from U.C. Berkeley. Tom can be reached on AppleLink at Tom.Chavez or on the InterNet at tomc@apple.com.

To change the maximum number of windows open on the desktop

- Type the new number into the "Max # of Windows" field

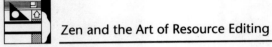

Chapter Four

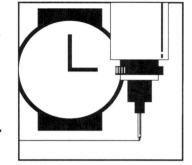

I Think Icon

by Derrick Schneider

*The old master held up a mouse
And blew from his palm,
Revealing the Source itself.
Look where the System hides the icon.*

I Think Icon

Icons are one of those things which make a Mac a Mac. Those little pictures which are so familiar are one of the core concepts and breakthroughs in the Macintosh interface. They serve to represent a concept quickly. Doesn't it make sense that you delete a file by putting it into the Trashcan? Icons in dialog boxes serve to bring your attention to the nature of the dialog. Even your hard drive and all floppy disks are shown by icons which uniquely identify them.

These icons, after a little while, can get boring. Sure the Trash can icon gets the point across, but don't you wish you could make it look like a paper shredder? I'm sure it comes as no surprise that *ResEdit* will let you do just that.

Figure 1 –

The ICN# and ICON resource picker icons.

Though all icons look alike to the user, there are actually four different types of black & white icons: ICN#, ICON, ics#, and SICN (the latter two being the small versions of the former). These terms are the names of the resources which contain these icons. So what's the difference? The basic difference is where the icons are used. ICN#s are used by the Finder and the Desktop file or by applications when a special object named a mask is needed (see below). ICONs are used within a program. For example, let's take a look at *HyperCard*. If you use *ResEdit* to open *HyperCard*, you will see both ICN# and ICON resources (see Figures 2 and 3). Open the ICN# resource (just look for now). You will see the two icons which you

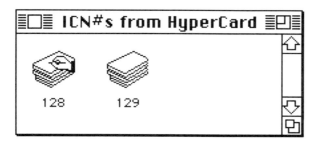

Figure 2 –
ICN#s from *Hypercard.*

see in the Finder: *HyperCard* itself and the icon for a stack. Now close this, and open the ICON resource. You will see all of the icons which you have probably seen when choosing an icon for a button.

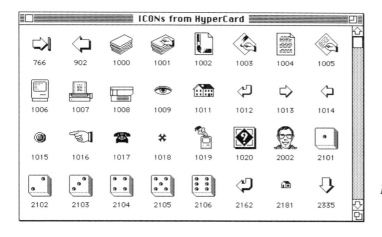

Figure 3 –
ICONs from *Hypercard.*

Editing icons

Now you know what the two types of icons are—so what? You probably want to go ahead and do something really cool to them, right? Okay, let's edit some icons. Make a copy of *HyperCard*. If you learn only one thing from this book, let it be that you should always work on a backup copy of a program when using *ResEdit*! Open your copy of HyperCard with *ResEdit*, and open the ICON resource (we'll get to the ICN# resource in a bit). You can

43

either edit an existing ICON, or choose Create New Resource from the Resource menu. In either case, you will get a window very much like that shown in Figure 4.

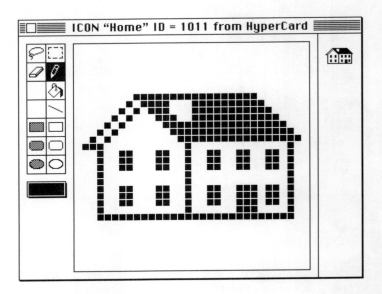

Figure 4 –
The ICON editor.

Now what? The icon editor features a simple selection of tools you can use to edit an icon. These are the same tools which are familiar from many of the available painting and drawing programs. There is also a pattern palette, which can be accessed by holding down the mouse button while clicking on the black rectangle below the tools. The palette will appear, and if you then move the mouse beyond its boundaries, it will "tear off." You then have a pattern palette you can put anywhere on your screen. Note that the "black rectangle" actually fills with whatever pattern you have selected currently. Make an icon, save your work, and you're done.

For more information about using these paint tools, read Appendix 3 – "A Quick Review of the Paint Tools."

ICN#s are a little bit different. To see why, open a copy of the Finder (or System if you're using System 7) with *ResEdit*, and then open the ICN# resource. Open the empty Trash can icon. This editor is bigger and has more views of the icon in a variety of situations. This is because ICN#s have some important differences from ICONs.

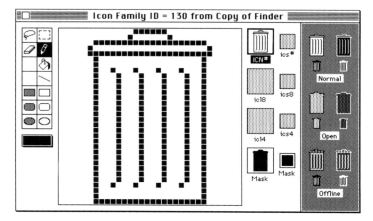

Figure 5 –
The ICN# editor.

The mask

So what's different about these two icons? What do ICN#s need that ICONs don't? I'll answer this with a question: What happens if you click once on an icon in the Finder? The icon usually becomes an inverse of itself, so that you know which icon you have selected. What happens to the folder icon if you open it? It becomes filled with a pattern, right? These things are all controlled by an ICN#'s mask, as it's called. This is the difference between the two types of icons.

In the good old days of the Macintosh, this mask could be edited so that when you clicked once on an icon in the Finder, it would look different. These were called "animated icons." For instance, some people might edit the mask of the folder icon so that if you selected it, it would look like an open folder. This is still possible in theory, but in reality Apple no longer supports animated icons. The mask, then, controls how the icon looks when selected. Some icons, when selected, look and act

45

considerably different than expected. A good example of this is *HD Backup*, which Apple provides with its system software. When you select this icon, it appears as if the two halves are not connected. This is because of the mask. If you click in certain spots between these halves, you'll notice that you can't move it. It's as if you're not clicking the icon at all. This is because of "holes" in the mask.

It was brought to my attention that ResEdit sometimes does not have enough memory to make a mask by the technique described here. If you find this is a problem for you, restart ResEdit and have as few windows open as possible. If it's still a problem, try increasing the memory allocation by choosing the ResEdit icon in the Finder, selecting Get Info... from the File menu, and changing the "Application Memory Size."

To create a mask, drag the image of the ICN# directly to the right of the editing area onto the panel which is labeled with the word "Mask." *ResEdit* will automatically create the necessary mask. If you do wish to experiment with how the mask works, you can bring up its editor by clicking once on the "Mask" panel. Or you may wish to edit the mask to fill in holes like those mentioned above.

At the right edge of the ICN# editor, you get to see how your icons look in a variety of situations. The first row, "Normal," shows your icon and its mask as they appear on the desktop in the Finder. The little tiny icons below it (ics#s) are used when viewing by small icon. Below that, you see a row labeled "Open." This is what the icons will look like when the file is open, e.g., and application open under MultiFinder. The third row, "Offline," shows what the icons will look like if the disk they are on has been ejected or unmounted.

Under *System 7*, icons used by the Finder are grouped into "families" so that all the icons the Finder uses (both color and black & white) can be accessed with the same ID number. Thus, if you have a color machine, you will notice several additions to the ICN# editor. These are the editing areas for the different members of the icon family, and you can copy an icon into them the same way you create a mask. Simply drag the icon into the panel of the other member of the family. The next section will cover color icons in more detail.

If you've edited the icon for an application and properly added the mask, you'll need to rebuild your

Desktop (hold down Command and Option when booting or inserting a disk) in order to see it. When the Finder
needs an icon to represent an application, it stores it in the
Desktop file so that it doesn't take as much time to retrieve
it. Even after editing your icon, the Finder will still look for
the icon in the old Desktop file. By rebuilding your
Desktop, you force the Finder to store your new icon in a
new Desktop file. An important note: If you have any
comments in the Get Info... dialog boxes in the Finder,
they will be erased when rebuilding the Desktop.

Editing around the office: icons you may want to edit

One of the most common icons which people edit is
the Trash can. Mine has gone through a whole range of
shapes: dumpster, shark, black hole, monsters, and Os-
car the Grouch. To edit this icon, open the Finder's (or
System's, if you're using System 7) icn#s. You will notice
that there are actually two Trash can icons; one used
when the Trash can is "empty" and the other used when
the Trash can is "full."

While you've got this window open, you'll see that all
the icons you're used to seeing in the Finder can be edited
here. However, one of these is a lie. Many people want to
edit the way a disk will look when it is inserted in the
drive, so they edit the floppy disk they see in the Finder.
However, this is to no avail. The icon for an inserted
floppy disk is built into the ROMs of your Macintosh. This
disk icon is actually used very seldomly. Well, it was worth
a shot, anyway.

Often, a person who feels comfortable editing icons
will go in search of the hard disk icon, so that he or she can
change it. Again, to no avail. This is usually not easily
done. The hard drive icon is frequently stored in the
hardware of the drive itself. Sometimes, you can find the

icon in the formatter for the drive (for instance, if you use SilverLining, it allows you to choose an icon for your hard drive) but that is rare, and it is not recommended that you change it even if it is there. For changing your hard disk icon, I recommend an INIT called *Façade*, which comes on the disk that is included with this book. This little program, by Greg Marriott, allows you to associate names of icons with names of disks. To change your hard disk icon, or the icon for specific floppies, open the file *FaçadeIcons*. Then find an icon you like (an ICN#) and change the name of the icon so that it matches the name of your hard drive or floppy disk. This is done through the Get Resource Info... dialog box within *ResEdit*. Make sure *Façade* and *FaçadeIcons* are in your System Folder, and restart your computer.

For more information about deciding where to put a resource, see Chapter 2, "Moving Resources."

Another type of icon that people look for is the custom icon for a folder in System 7. When you paste an icon onto a folder, the System makes an invisible file named "Icon" within that folder. ResEdit is able to see this file and open it.

If you wish to add icons to *HyperCard*, you can do so by opening the resource fork of the stack you wish to put them in. If it is a new stack, *ResEdit* will probably tell you that the stack has no resource fork, and you're about to create one. Don't worry about this. It just means that no extra resources have been added yet. Keep in mind that if you're going to distribute a stack with an extra icon (one not supplied by *HyperCard*), the icon needs to be placed in the resource fork of the stack itself. That way, the icon will always be available. Remember that icons used within stacks are ICONs, and not ICN#s.

Icon overview

To get to the icon resources:

- Open *ResEdit* and open the file you wish to look at
- Double-click on either the ICN# or ICON icon
- Double-click on the icon you wish to change

To create a mask for an ICN#:

- Click and hold the mouse button on the icon in the "Icon" or "ICN#" panel
- Drag this icon to the panel which says "Mask"

Chapter Five

Color Icons

by Lisa Lee

Many times the icons have turned from
green to yellow –
So much for the capricious earth!
Dust in your eyes, the triple world is narrow;
Nothing on your mind, your screen is wide enough

Color Icons

Color icons have been around since Apple first unveiled the Macintosh II. The new possibilities of color introduced many new resources to deal with beyond black & white. Among these new resources was the cicn, short for Color ICoN. However, it was not used very effectively. Editing cicns required programs other than *ResEdit*, and placing them on the desktop required still more programs, outside of the system software. *ResEdit* now has editors for cicns, and you can use this to add color icons to menus or dialog boxes. The editors for the cicn is exactly like the ones we're going to describe here.

For *System 7*, Apple has created two new types of color icon resources, the icl and ics. The two are very closely related (icl is the large icon, and ics is the small icon) and each one is split into two parts. icls are split into icl8s and icl4s, which are for 8-bit (256 colors) and 4-bit (16 colors) monitors, respectively. Similarly, ics resources are either ics8 or ics4. In the *System 6.0.x* series, these new icons are not seen by the System (see below for installing them onto your desktop under *System 6*). However, *System 7* recognizes these resources without the use of any additional programs.

Icons are now divided into families, which means that you no longer have to create separate resources; they are created automatically.

The icl and ics editors

To see what an icl looks like, set your computer to either 256 colors or 16 colors, depending on how many you have available. Use *ResEdit* to open a copy of the System file. *System 6* does not have the icl8 resources installed. In order to see what one looks like, use the Create New Resource… command from the Resource menu. You will see a dialog box like the one shown in Figure 1.

In the field, type the word icl8 (if you're set to 256 colors) or icl4 (if you're set to 16 colors). Press <Return> and you will see the editor shown in Figure 2.

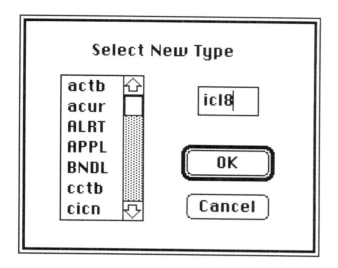

Figure 1 –
The Create New Resource… dialog box.

Using the icl editor

The most prominent feature of this window is the FatBits window showing the color icon. Along the left of the window is the area filled with all the familiar paint tools. There is one new tool, the color dropper, which is

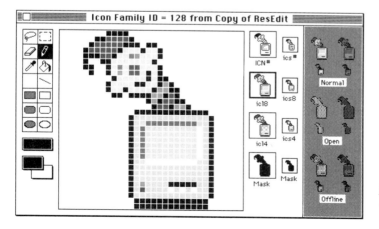

Figure 2 –
The icl editor.

described below. Below this, you will see the selection of colors (as a pop-up, tear-off palette). These can be changed by choosing a set from the Color menu. "Standard 256 Colors" gives you access to all the colors in the System palette. The "Apple Icon Colors" option gives you access to 34 colors which Apple reccommends for use in icons. You will also see the pattern palette, which is very similar to the one in black & white editors. Directly to the right of the editing area, you can see the actual-size icons for icl8s, ics8s, ics#s, icl4s, ics4s, and ICN#s (ic#s are the new version of small icons for ICN#s), as well as the mask which is responsible for all of them. If you click on each of these, the individual editor for that icon will be brought forward. This provides a quick way to toggle between the different types of icons used in the Finder. To the far right, you can get an idea of how your icons will look in a variety of situations. In each of these sections, the normal icon is on the right side and the selected icon is on the left side. "Normal" shows you what the icon looks like when sitting patiently on the desktop. "Open" shows you the icon when it is opened on the desktop. "Offline" shows you what the icons look like if they are still visible when the disk they are on is ejected. Note that each of these will only show what the current icon will look like. If you are editing an icl8 and wish to see how the icl4 looks, simply click on the icl4 icon to the right of the editing area, and *ResEdit* will re-adjust the views.

Those are the basics of the icl resources. ics resources are exactly the same, except for the fact that the editing area is a little bit smaller (a 16 x 16 grid as opposed to the full 32 x 32 grid for an icon). The paint tools for color editors are a little bit different than for black & white icons, and those will be described now.

The new color tools

The most radical difference between the color paint tools and the black & white tools is the color dropper, shown as a small eyedropper. This tool can be very useful, especially when using 256 colors. If you click with the color dropper on a pixel, the color will be set to the color of the pixel you have clicked on. Thus, if you are creating an icon and you wish the upper right to be the same color as the lower left, but can't quite tell which shade of gray you used in the lower left, simply click on the lower left with the color dropper. Then you can color in the upper right area.

This leads to the next new tool, the pencil. In a black & white editor, using the pencil to click on a pixel does one of two things: turns it off or on, depending on its initial state. In a color editor, this is a little bit different. If you click on a pixel which is different color than the selected color, the pixel you have clicked will become that color. If, however, you click on a pixel which is the same color as the currently selected color, that pixel will become white. If you want to use the color dropper while using the pencil tool, press the Option key while the pencil tool is active, and the pencil tool will turn into the color dropper. Release the option key and the tool reverts to the pencil.

All the paint tools except the eraser use the selected color. The eraser makes everything white. Double-clicking on the eraser clears the FatBits window.

Installing your new icons: System 6

To use your color icons on the desktop, you should use a program called *SunDesk*, by Frédéric Miserey (included on this disk). To use it, do the following:

First, open the file *SunDesk Icons*. Second, use *ResEdit* to open the Desktop file (you cannot be under MultiFinder when you do this). Click once on the ICN# icon in the Desktop file, and choose Copy from the Edit menu. Then go to the *SunDesk Icons* window and choose Paste from the Edit menu. That will provide you with the icons from your desktop. Note: *SunDesk* will only work if the number of ICN#s equals the number of icl8s in the *SunDesk Icons* file. So don't copy all icons from the desktop into the *SunDesk Icons* file, otherwise your color icons will not appear on your desktop.

Open up the ICN# you wish to colorize, and make icl8s and icl4s by dragging the ICN# to the icl8 and icl4 panel, to the right of the editing area. Then use the tools described above to color this icon. Important: Do not change the shape of the icon itself! You can color its edges and insides, but do not color beyond the edges of the icon itself. If you do, the icon will not look good, because the mask will not have been altered to accommodate the new shape.

Save your changes, make sure the files are where they are supposed to be (i.e., in the System Folder), and restart you Macintosh. You will then see your new color icons.

You can change icons for other applications and documents by replacing the icl resource in the application with the newly created icon made in *ResEdit*. Many applications use ID number 128 for their icon, so if you have a large library of color icons (as in *SunDesk*), you will need to change the resource ID number of the icon you want to use to match the ID number of the icon you want to replace. If you just want to alter an application's icon (e.g., make it fatter or thinner), you will have to follow the same resource ID renumbering procedure if you want the color icon to appear on your desktop.

System 7

Create your color icon resources with *ResEdit* by opening the application and creating a new icl8. Color it to suit your taste. When you restart, rebuild the Desktop by holding the Command and Option keys when starting up. Your color icons will now be used whenever you have your Mac showing colors. You do not need to use extensions such as *SunDesk* or *ColorFinder* to have color icons to appear on your desktop with *System 7*.

You can view your icl or ics resources in any Finder window via the Views Control Panel. First, double-click on your hard drive icon or on a folder. Select one of the List views from the View menu in the Finder (Name, Size, Kind, Date, etc.), then open the Views Control Panel via the Control Panels in the Apple menu. Select one of the three icon shapes you would like to see in selected windows which are in list view mode. Windows in list view will automatically display the new icon size.

Also, if you put anything in the Apple Menu Items folder in the System Folder, the System will use the appropriate ics resource if it's available. If an application or DA is chosen, the System again uses an ics for the Application menu, if an ics is available.

An alternate way to install color icons is to paste them directly onto the file or folder (which can also have a custom icon). To do this, make your artwork in *ResEdit*, or in your favorite paint program. Select the actual image (not the resource, but the actual pixels from the editor) and copy it to the Clipboard. Next, go to the Finder and click once on the file or folder you want to customize. Choose Get Info... from the Edit menu, and click on the icon at the top of the dialog box. Now paste your image from the Clipboard. Now, that file or folder will have that icon. While this is good for individual files, if you want all the files from a program to be in color, you need to use *ResEdit* to edit the icon families.

For more information about how these icons work, read "Getting a Running Start with System 7."

Some tips on creating color icons

- Try to sketch out what the icon will look like on regular paper before sitting down in front of your Macintosh. Try not to create the icon pixel-by-pixel. Instead, try to draw as if your mouse were a normal writing instrument like a pen or pencil. I find it easier to create the original icon in black & white, and as I add color, modify the icon until it looks usable.

- Experiment with different colors. Don't feel a need to stick to colors that are physically located near to one another. Try to visually match the shade of a color you like (or try to imagine the color you would like to use in your mind) and find the matching color on the palette.

- Once you have a rough outline of the icon, you can move the whole image or parts of it with the marquee tool. If the marquee tool is double-clicked, the whole image is selected in the icon creation window and you can position it anywhere within the icon window.

- When you are finished with the icon, be sure to choose Remove Unused Colors from the Color menu. When *ResEdit* first creates the icon, it includes all the available colors in the icon, taking up unnecessary memory. This menu command will remove all the colors you did not use when making the icon. This is only true for cicns; icon families reserve a fixed amount of memory.

- Always make sure, if you have an 8-bit computer, to make 4-bit icons as well. That way your desktop will still be in color if you switch to 16 colors or if you give your artwork to a friend who uses 16 colors. You can create lighter color shades for 4-bit icons (similar to 8-bit shades) by using dot patterns in the pop-up pattern menu located just above the color selection pop-up menu.

Lisa Lee has been a BMUG member since 1989 and helped create the BMUG movie for the 1990 Macworld Expo booth in San Francisco. Lisa has also co-coordinated the BMUG Multimedia SIG and is in the process of creating more color animation and original music. She is a U.C. Berkeley graduate and can be reached on America Online at LisaL1BMUG.

- If you're using *SunDesk*, and you do use someone else's icls, be sure to use the Get Resource Info… dialog box to match the ID numbers. When you create an original piece of art, *ResEdit* will make sure that all the members of the icon family have the same resource number. However, other Systems may have different IDs, in which case *SunDesk* will not recognize them as being associated with your black & white icons.

Color icon overview

(icl8s used for examples, though the same is true for icl4s, ics8s, ics4s, and ics#s)

To add icl8s to a file which does not have any:

- Open *ResEdit*, and use it to open the file you wish to add an icl8 to
- Choose Create New Resource… from the Resource menu
- Type the letters icl8, and hit Return

To add icl8s to a file which only has ICN#s (visible on color Macs only):

- Double-click on the ICN# icon you wish to colorize
- Click and drag the icon in the "ICN#" panel to the "icl8" panel
- Color in the icl8 as you wish

To change between editors in an icon family:

- Click on the panel you wish to edit (e.g., the "icl8" panel to edit icl8s)

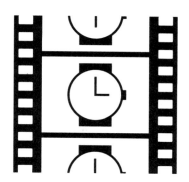

Chapter Six

Cursor Resources

by Rick Reynolds

The watch is the same old watch,
The I-beams exactly as they were,
Yet I've become the thingness
Of all the cursors I see!

Cursor Resources

There are two kinds of resources which determine the appearance of your cursor on the screen: CURS and acur.

These two resources are used on different occasions. The CURS resource determines the physical appearance of a cursor. The acur resource is used to animate a cursor when your Macintosh is busy executing a command so that you get some signal that your Macintosh is working on something and not just crashed.

Both of these resources are designed to be modular in nature, meaning that you can change them much like changing the compact disc in your CD player or the clothes on your Barbie Doll.

ResEdit allows you to alter these resources to produce interesting effects. With it, you can design your own watch cursor, and replace the one which comes with the Finder. If you're not artistically inclined, you don't need to design these resources yourself. You can download them from networks, borrow them from other applications, or get them from your friends. Then all you have to do is quickly insert them into the resource fork of the application.

Getting our hands dirty

Let's take a look at these resources. Use *ResEdit* to open a copy of the Finder. Open up the CURS resource in the Finder by double-clicking on it.

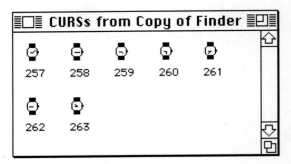

Figure 1 –

The animated watch cursor, frame by frame.

The items in the window in Figure 1 are the various CURS resources and their numerical designations. Each CURS can have its own name, but the Macintosh operating system tracks these resources by number, not name. Clicking once on one of these CURS resources will select it, so that you can copy or cut the resource onto the Clipboard for later use within *ResEdit*. You can also access the Get Resource Info… menu command to change the cursor's ID number and name. To get to the CURS editor, double-click on a single CURS resource.

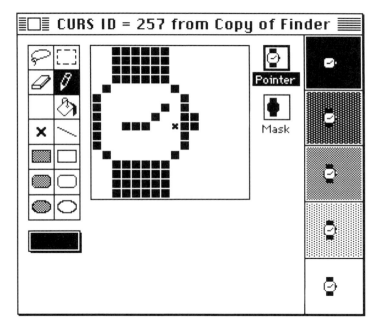

Figure 2 –
The CURS editor in *ResEdit*.

The CURS editor, as you may have noticed, is very similar to other editors for graphic resources. The biggest part of the editor is the editing area, which shows the selected cursor, enlarged for easy editing. To the left of this is the area where you choose a painting tool. Directly below this is the pattern palette (the black rectangle), which can be pulled off and moved to a convenient place. To see it, hold down the mouse button over the rectangle.

For more information about paint tools, see Appendix 1 – "A Quick Review of the Paint Tools."

63

Directly to the right of the editing area are two small windows, "Pointer" and "Mask." With these small windows, you can quickly move between the cursor and mask editors. (For more information about cursor masks, see below.) At the far right of the window, *ResEdit* shows your cursor on a variety of different patterns.

The hot spot of a cursor

All cursors have a single pixel which is "the hot spot"—the point where the action takes place when you click the mouse button. Think about the arrow cursor for a minute. When you click on an object (such as a close box or an icon) with the tip of the pointer, something usually happens. What would happen if you clicked on something with the base of the arrow (the thin part)? Nothing would happen. This is because the hot spot of the arrow is at the very tip. Therefore, no matter how big your cursor is, the Macintosh is only concerned with a single pixel, the hot spot.

To create a new hot spot within a cursor, choose the hot spot tool (it looks like an X). Then, click in the editing area to place it. That's all there is to it!

There are some design tips which you should follow, however. When placing a hot spot, it's important that the user can easily know where it is, even if they don't know what a hot spot is. Some examples of good places are at the end of a pointed area (as in the arrow), in the middle of crosshairs, or in the center of a symmetric shape (the center of a circle, for instance).

Another design tip that is useful for animated cursors such as the watch is that you should make the location of the hot spot consistent. In the watch, for example, it would be strange if the hot spot were placed at the end of the moving hand in each frame; the cursor would appear to swirl around. Instead, you could put it on the "dial" of the watch (or slightly to the right, as Apple did). The important thing is that you don't keep changing it.

The mask

Cursor resources, like icon families, have an attribute known as a mask. In ICN#s, the mask controls how the icon looks when selected or open, as well as how it looks against various backgrounds. With cursors, the mask is only responsible for how the cursor looks when seen on a background. Creating a mask is very simple. Drag the image from the "Pointer" area into the "Mask" area, and *ResEdit* will create the appropriate mask.

Sometimes, however, this mask may not be perfect. For instance, look again at Figure 2. Look at the cursor on the black background, and you will see that the only visible part of the cursor is the face. To fix this, you can edit the mask. Click once on the "Mask" window to bring up the mask editor. Now, surround the cursor with a line one pixel thick. Your watch is now completely visible on a black background. Incidentally, this is what happens when you place the black arrow cursor on a black background. The mask keeps it visible.

As you are designing, it often helps to try out your cursor. Try Cursor, from the CURS menu, that appears only while you are in the CURS editor, allows you to work with the new CURS resource. This menu selection is actually a toggle switch which activates the animation until it is turned off. When you wish to stop the animation, simply choose this menu option again. Note: Under MultiFinder or System 7, you will only have the new cursor within *ResEdit*. If you switch applications, your cursor switches to the resource fork of the active application. Your cursor will also revert if you go to another window in *ResEdit*. You will have to replace the Finder in your System Folder with the copy you've been editing, and restart your Mac, to see the new cursor in all applications.

With your new knowledge, you can easily add single cursors (non-animated) to any application. You can also edit existing cursors if you wish. Adding new cursors won't usually do anything, since the program doesn't know how to use more than its own cursors. However, *HyperCard* will let you show an original cursor from a script. Refer to your instruction manual for more information on how to do this.

acurs: Animating your cursor

In System 7, the watch cursors all have different IDs from the ones shown here. Nonetheless, the techniques for editing them are the same.

When you issue a time-consuming command on your Macintosh, you usually see some sort of animated cursor, telling you that the Macintosh is still active but busy. This animation sequence is controlled by the acur resource (Animated CURsor). To get an idea of how this works, open the acur resource in a copy of the Finder.

```
┌─────────────────────────────────────────────────────────┐
│ ▤□▦▦▦▦▦    acur ID = 0 from Copy of Finder    ▦▦▦ │⇧│
│                                                         │ │
│   Number of        ┌──────────────────┐                │ │
│   "frames"         │ 8                │                │ │
│   (cursors)        └──────────────────┘                │ │
│                                                         │ │
│   Used a           ┌──────────────────┐                │ │
│   "frame"          │ 0                │                │ │
│   counter          └──────────────────┘                │ │
│                                                         │ │
│     1) *****                                            │ │
│                    ┌──────────────────┐                │ │
│     'CURS'         │ 4                │                │ │
│     Resource Id    └──────────────────┘                │ │
│                                                         │ │
│     2) *****                                            │ │
│                    ┌──────────────────┐                │ │
│     'CURS'         │ 257              │                │▽│
│     Resource Id    └──────────────────┘                │⊡│
└─────────────────────────────────────────────────────────┘
```

Figure 3 –
The acur editor.

The acur editor provides you with a lot of areas to look at. The values in this window can be changed as if you were in a word processor. The first field, Number of "frames" (cursors), is the field which determines how many frames are in the animated cursor. In the watch cursor, there are eight frames.

The second field is the number of ticks (60ths of a second) between frames of the animated cursor. If you wish to slow your cursor down for visual effect, change this number. Normally, it is left at 0, with no time between frames. You will need to play with this number to determine the appropriate number for your particular cursor.

To change how quickly your animated cursor appears during time-consuming operations, see page 44.

The rest of the fields describe the order in which the frames are shown, so that the sequence is correct. Note that the first field uses CURS ID# 4, which doesn't exist in the Finder. This field actually calls a cursor from the System file. There is one cursor in the System file that can be called by all applications, not just the Finder. That way, even if the application doesn't have an animated cursor sequence, it can call up this resource to indicate that it is busy.

As an alternative to *ResEdit*'s rather bland acur editor, you may want to look at Christopher Reed's acur editor, included on the disk which comes with this book. Follow the instructions that come with it, and you'll have a much nicer, much more intuitive editor for your animated cursors. It's graphically oriented, so it's far easier to work with than *ResEdit*'s. For more information about installing new editors, read Appendix 3, "Installing Editors." Figure 4 gives you an idea of how much nicer this editor is.

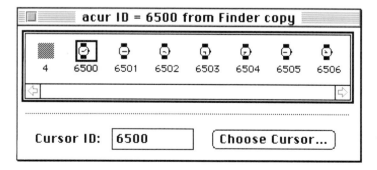

Figure 4 –
Chris Reed's acur editor.

Creating your own watch cursor

Creating your own watch cursor involves several steps. The first steps are to create the cursors which will be used. Use the Create New Resource… menu command to create new frames for editing. Then use the paint tools to create your CURS resources.

The next step is to create a new acur resource, which will generate the animation. Again, use Create New Resource… to make an acur resource. To enter new frames, click once on a row of asterisks (you will understand when you see it), and choose Insert New Field.

CursorAnimator: A quick alternative

It can be very time-consuming to edit watch cursors. Even if you edit the Finder's watch cursor to something you really like, you may open an application to discover that is has its own animated sequence. This means that you have to edit this one as well.

There is a very good shareware program called *CursorAnimator* (on the disk included with this book), which allows you to load cursors into memory, and then replace all watch cursors with the same animation sequence. To use it, you have to have two things in a resource file: the necessary CURS resources, and the acur resource. The program (which is accessed through the Contol Panel) then gives you the option of opening this file. When you open the file, *Cursor Animator* shows you a name, which is chosen from the acur resource. As a result, you need to have an acur resource even if you're adding a non-animated cursor, so that your cursor will have a name.

Rick Reynolds, among many other activities, is the executive director of the Bay Area NeXT User Group (BANG). Rick has a color pre-press service bureau in San Francisco and is a contributing editor for NeXTWORLD Magazine.

Cursor overview

To get to the actual cursors in a program:

- Open *ResEdit*, and use it to open the file you wish to alter, usually a copy of the Finder
- Double-click on the CURS resource icon

To get to the animation sequence:

- Open *ResEdit*, and use it to open the file you wish to alter
- Double-click on the acur resource

To change the "hot spot" of a cursor:

- Open the specific CURS resource you wish to alter (e.g., CURS 128)
- Choose the hot spot tool (an "X") from the tool area
- Click on the pixel you wish to be the hot spot

To make a mask of a cursor:

- Click and drag the cursor from the "Cursor" panel to the "Mask" panel

To temporarily work with the cursor you have created:

- Choose Try Cursor from the CURS menu

To make an animation sequence:

- Open the acur resource you wish to alter
- Set "Number of Frames" to the number of frames in your animation sequence
- In each "CURS Resource ID" field, type the appropriate ID number of the CURS resource which is to be used for this frame

Chapter Seven

Menus and You

by Steve Yaste

The Apple menu's aflame with bright color,
But File is steeped in snow.
Such are a Zen-man's menus –
The menu bar survives all earthly fire.

Menus and you

Menus are one of the most commonly used things in a Macintosh program. It is through the menus that nearly all the functionality of a good Macintosh program is reached.

An important part of the Macintosh philosophy is that menus have a consistent look and feel for users. That is the reason all programs are mandated (in Apple's "Human Interface Design Guidelines") to have, as their first three menus, the Apple, File, and Edit menus. Further, there are certain defined menu items which must appear in these menus (such as Quit and Undo) and 12 pt. Chicago text is specified for all menu text.

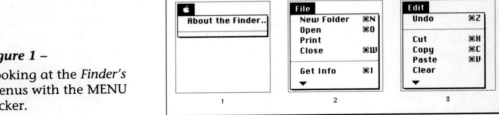

Figure 1 –
Looking at the *Finder's* menus with the MENU picker.

However, these menus can be boring. Every Macintosh menu looks basically the same: 12 pt. Chicago type in a long column running down the page. Sometimes it would be nice to have a variety of colors, or some icons. *ResEdit* allows you to make many interesting changes to a menu. Use *ResEdit* to open a copy of the Finder, and look at the menus which are there. If you're using System 7, the menus in the Finder are not MENU resources, so you have to open a copy of your favorite application instead, but you'll still be able to follow along.

The MENU editor

Figure 2 shows the menu editor for MENU ID = 5 from the Finder. Looking over this window, we see the currently selected menu and the items in it. The selected element (either the menu name or individual item) is highlighted. In this sample, the menu name is "Special," and six menu items are listed.

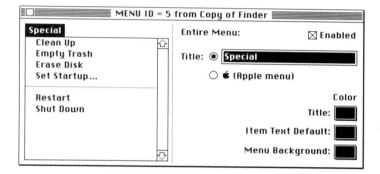

Figure 2 –

Editing the menu title in *ResEdit's* MENU editor.

The right-hand side of the MENU editor shows the details of the selected resource item. In the case of this sample, the entire menu has been selected by clicking the menu's title "Special," on the left hand side. The "Enabled" check box allows you to specify whether the menu should initially be displayed as grayed-out (disabled) or normal. Below that, you can see the Title field with the Apple menu radio button. These allow a person to easily specify a menu resource in his or her application as the Apple menu, or to give it the name which will be used in the program.

On color systems, the menu color controls are below. You can individually specify different colors for the Menu Title, Item Text, and Menu Background. The Menu Background Color only affects the backgrounds of individual menus, not the menu bar itself. Also note that the Item Text Color in Figure 2, above, is a default and will affect each of the menu's items; however, you can override these defaults for any particular menu item.

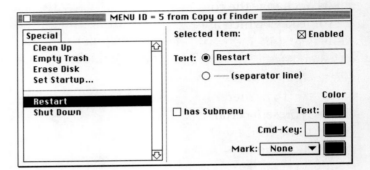

Figure 3 –
Editing a menu item.

In Figure 3, above, you can see the same MENU resource, but now a particular menu item has been selected on the left, and a few things have changed. The editor now says "Selected Item" rather than "Entire Menu." Now that you have selected an item, all the changes made in the editor will affect that menu item only. As in the case of editing the entire menu, individual menu items may be grayed out as well. The Title box has changed to the Item Text box, and the radio button allows you to define this item as a separator line. (Separator lines can also be defined by entering a hyphen as the item text.)

One very useful field in this editor is the "Cmd-Key" field. This allows you to set which command key you would like to be associated with that particular menu item. Command keys can often speed up work and productivity. However, before you go adding command-keys to every single menu option, there are some things to keep in mind. Perhaps the most obvious and the most common mistake is from a technical standpoint: Don't make one key the command-key equivalent for two or more menu items. There actually is a procedure the Macintosh follows in this case (the rightmost menu, or the lowest menu item if both command keys are in one menu, gets the priority), but don't do it. If you want to do something like make 'E' the command-key equivalent for Empty Trash, then delete or change the command-key for Eject Disk. There are some keys which are rarely used for command-key equivalents, including numbers and punctuation, letters such as R, U, T, J, K, and others. If you're going to delete command keys, keep in mind that Apple standards say that there are certain keys which should always represent certain menu options. Figure 4, below, shows some of these common command-key equivalents. Do not change these, as someone else using the machine or program will become confused.

A	Select All	C	Copy	F	Find
N	New	O	Open	P	Print
Q	Quit	S	Save	V	Paste
W	Close	X	Cut	Z	Undo

Figure 4 –
Some standard command-keys and their usual meanings.

The other factor is the interface issue: command keys should be easy to find. If you have ß as your command-key equivalent, are you really going to remember that your command-key equivalent is Option-S? Likewise, will someone else using your program or your computer know this?

On color machines, there are controls for the colors of the menu item which has been selected.

At any point, you can see how your menu looks by pulling down the sample menu in the menu bar. It will be surrounded by a rectangle to differentiate it from the other menus. It will show you all of the text, command-keys and colors.

By now, you are no doubt wondering when I'm going to get to the subject of icons. Let's look again at the Special menu from the Finder. The command for attaching an icon to a menu item is found in the MENU menu of *ResEdit*, which is only available when you're in the MENU editor. Select the Choose Icon... item and you will be presented with the dialog on the previous page. Note: When working on the Finder, you should be aware that an unaltered Finder won't have any ICON resources in it. You'll need to import or create them in order to use icons in the Finder.

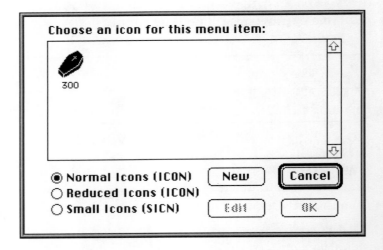

Figure 5 –

The icon picker for menu bar items.

The Choose Icon dialog works with three types of resources: ICONs, reduced ICONs, and SICNs. ICONs are resource types that date back to the original Macintosh resource set. Reduced icons are exactly the same as ICONs, except that the original 32x32 ICON is reduced to a 16x16 size. SICN's, on the other hand, are relatively new resource types which are designed to allow the developer to have more control over the appearance of the smaller 16x16 size icon. You can select which of these three icon types you want to use in your program by clicking on one of the three radio buttons on the left side of the window. In order for *ResEdit* to use an

For more information about editing icons, see Chapter 4 – "I Think Icon."

icon for a menu, it must have an ID number between 257 and

511. Reset this as needed with the Get Resource Info... dialog box under the Resource menu. For now, just select the Normal Icons radio button. Just to the right of the radio buttons are four control buttons: New, Edit, OK, and Cancel. OK and Cancel function the usual way, and the New and Edit buttons are related to the icons themselves. Both of these buttons will show the ICON editor, either blank (for new icons) or filled with the icon (for editing icons). For more information about how to use this editor, see the ICON section earlier in this book. Once you have completed your editing, select the OK button to save the ICON into the MENU. Again, you can see how your menu will look by pulling down the sample menu at the far right of the menu bar in the MENU editor. If you wish to edit this ICON further at some later date, you may edit it either from the MENU editor, or by opening and selecting the proper ICON resource directly. Please note that if you select the Reduced Icon radio button and then Edit, you will actually be editing the full-sized version of the selected ICON.

If you later decide that you no longer want to have an icon associated with your menu item, simply re-open the proper menu resource, select the menu item with the icon you wish to delete, and then select Remove Icon from the MENU menu.

If you wish to have a color icon associated with a menu, you must first add a black & white icon to a menu. Then add a cicn which has the same ID number as the black & white icon.

For more information about color icons, see Chapter 5 – Color Icons.

Adding new menu fonts

If you wish to put your menus into a different font than Chicago 12, you have to use a different resource known as the FOND resource. This is described more thoroughly in the section about fonts, by Jens Peter Alfke, and you should refer to that article, since there are a number of guidelines and pitfalls associated with that.

For more information about fonts, see Chapter 9 – "Everything You've Always Wanted to Know About Fonts."

More technical stuff: submenus and the rest of the MENU menu

When Apple introduced System 5.0, the Human Interface Design Group added the ability to have hierarchical menus in applications and on the desktop. Many people have seen hierarchical menus in their favorite word processors or paint programs (See Figure 6, below). While you won't be able to add functional sub-menus to your favorite commercial applications, you will be able to use *ResEdit* to easily define them for any applications you write.

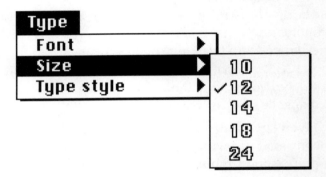

Figure 7 –
A hierarchical menu.

If you look again at Figure 3, you will see that there is a check box next to the words "Has Submenu." If this box is not checked, there is no submenu for this item. If this check box is set, however, a new field will appear: "ID:." To use a submenu for a menu, you must enter the ID number of the menu resource you wish to use as the submenu. If you have not defined this submenu, you must be sure to enter an ID# that is different from any other menu ID#s. Defining the items for this submenu is done exactly the same way as defining items for a primary menu. Notice that when you create this new ID number, it will be assigned the name of its parent item (or a shortened version). In order to help keep things straight, it is recommended that you not change this name, even though it can only be seen with *ResEdit*.

There are a couple of useful things you should know about editing submenus. If you're looking at a menu item which uses a submenu, you can double-click on the menu item (within the list on the left-hand side) to bring the submenu forward. This can be handy if you wish to look at the submenu quickly. Another aspect of submenus is that command-key equivalents cannot be assigned to menu items with submenus. This makes sense for two main reasons. First, what would happen if they did have a command-key equivalent? When a user used the command key, what would the application do? Show the submenu? Second, there is no room for the command key on the right side of the menu. For these reasons, *ResEdit* will not even present the "Cmd-Key" field to you if the check box next to "Has Submenu" is checked.

Occasionally when creating a program, you might wish to reorder the menu items so that their order makes more sense. Menu items can very easily be reordered merely by selecting the item you want to move, holding down the mouse button, and dragging the menu item to its new position. This should only be done by people writing their own programs, however, since rearranging the menu items is the same as changing the text of all of them: Menu item 1 will always perform the same command, even if it has the same wording as menu item 2.

The MENU menu can also be used to return any menu or menu item to the default black & white color scheme by selecting the menu title or menu item and then choosing the Use Default Colors menu item. The last item to discuss in this menu is the Edit Menu & MDEF ID... item. This brings up a new dialog which allows you to enter a new resource ID number and a new MDEF (Menu DEFinition) number. Each MENU resource has two ID#s. One is the resource ID# that we have already talked about and is generally assigned by *ResEdit* when you create a new menu resource. The second is the MDEF ID number set inside the MENU editor. This number is only used by the Toolbox menu management routines, and while it is not required that they be the same, life will certainly be easier if they are.

The MDEF number is generally '0,' which is the number of the default System MDEF Proc, the standard pull-down menu. The only time that this might be different is when your application has non-standard menus such as palettes or ICON bars. Unless you are writing a program and have created unique, non-standard menu definitions, it is highly recommended that you not alter this ID#.

What can I do with these resources?

Steve Yaste is the Manager of Software Testing for Power Up! Software in San Mateo, California. In a previous life Steve worked at Apple Computer, Inc. coordinating and supervising the software testing of Macintosh CPUs. Besides working on most of the Macintosh II-class projects through the IIfx, Steve worked on 32-bit QuickDraw and several video cards. Previous to his experience at Apple, Steve has worked on testing products such as Filemaker II (Forethought, Inc.) and dBase III and dBase developers release.

Now that we have the theoretical information behind menus, what sort of practical applications can this information be used for? One of the most useful applications is adding command-key equivalents to commonly-used menu items. Software companies cannot anticipate the needs of every single person who uses their product. As a result, a menu command which you frequently use may not have a command key to activate it. You are then forced to mouse around to the menu and the menu item, which can take a lot of time if most of the work for the program is done from the keyboard, as in a word processor. With *ResEdit*, however, you can quickly assign a command key, as described above.

Although icons in menus may seem frivolous, they can be a valuable educational tool. If a person is not sure what a certain menu item does, a well-designed icon next to the command can eliminate a lot of confusion. This is especially useful if you are creating *HyperCard* stacks with *HyperCard 2.x*, since you can create menus and then insert them into the menu bar when needed.

With these tools, you can do quite a bit to customize your menus to suit your own needs and the needs of others. However, there are some things to watch out for when doing this. If you are using *Microsoft Word*, you will not be able to modify the menus with *ResEdit*, as *Word* codes its own menus into the menu bar. *Word* does allow you to change menus, but it is from within the program itself. Please consult your instruction manual for more information on how to do this. Similarly, the software for America Online does not use standard menus, although there is some limited editing power accessible from within the program.

If you use *System 7*, and go hunting for the menus in the Finder, you will be disappointed. *System 7* uses a new type of resource for this, the fmnu (short for Finder MeNU). It is difficult to edit this resource, since it does not open as a MENU resource. There are some tips for dealing with them, however, in the "Getting a Running Start with System 7" section later in this book.

MENU overview

To get to the MENU resource:

- Open *ResEdit*
- In *ResEdit*, open the program you wish to alter
- Double-click on the MENU icon

To change an aspect of the entire menu:

- In the MENU resource, open the menu you wish to modify
- Make sure that the editor says "Entire Menu:"
- If you wish to change the name of the menu, type the new name into the "Title:" field
- If you wish to make this menu the Apple menu, click on the button next to the Apple symbol

- To change the various colors of the menu, hold the mouse button down on the square next to the color you wish to change. Once the color palette appears, choose the color you would like

To change a menu item:

- Open the MENU resource you would like to change
- Click once on the menu item you wish to alter
- To change the text, type the new text into the "Text:" field
- To make this item into a separator line, click on the button next to the dotted line
- To change or add a command key, type the new command key into the "Cmd-Key:" field
- To attach a submenu, click on the "Has Submenu" box and then type in the ID number of the menu which is to be the submenu
- To change a color attribute, hold the mouse button down over the square next to the appropriate area. When the palette appears, choose the color you would like to use
- To add a mark to a menu item, hold down the mouse button on the "Mark" pop-up menu and choose the mark you wish to add

To add an icon to a menu:

- Go to the menu item you wish to attach an icon to
- Select Choose Icon… from the MENU menu
- Select the icon you wish to attach
- Use "New" or "Edit" to create a new icon or edit an existing one

Chapter Eight

Pattern Resources

by Derrick Schneider

Four patterns each:
a cup of tea,
the scroll bar.

Pattern resources

Patterns are one of the more subtle resources in the Macintosh operating system. They are always there, but very few people notice them consciously. The average Mac user has his or her desktop pattern set to gray (the default) and never thinks twice about it. You can change the desktop pattern with the General control panel, but this is time-consuming, and most of the patterns Apple provides are not very nice to look at for long periods of time. People with color Macs may have discovered that the General control panel does have an editor for making a color desktop pattern, but few people bother to change it. Another more subtle pattern is in the scroll bar, but this can't be changed in the Control Panel.

What the system software lacks, *ResEdit* can make up for easily. With *ResEdit*, you can change many common patterns easily, including the desktop pattern and the scroll bar pattern. On a Mac II family machine, your desktop pattern can be substantially larger than the 8x8 pixels the General control panel allows. You can even change the patterns within *ResEdit* itself, or the built-in patterns that you can access from the General control panel.

The PAT Editor

To start learning about patterns, make a copy of your System and open it with *ResEdit*. Open up the PAT resource (which is actually spelled 'PAT '), and take a look for a second. You'll notice that each of the samples is a small swatch of that particular pattern. PAT#16 is the current desktop pattern, and PAT#17 is the scroll bar pattern. Double-click on PAT#17, and you'll see the PAT editor.

This editor has all the tools common to *ResEdit*. For more information about using these tools, see Appendix 1, "A Quick Review of the Paint Tools." The main window is divided into two areas. The left area contains an 8x8 editing area where you can actually edit the pixels in the pattern. The right area shows you a sample of the pattern as it will actually look. The Mac makes patterns by taking your 8x8 image and repeating it over and over again. You can make this pattern as garish as you'd like, or as nice.

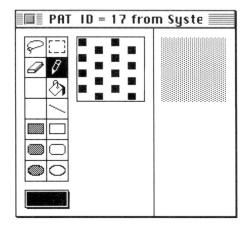

Figure 1-
PAT editor with PAT 17 open.

Within the editor, you have a PAT menu which allows you to try the pattern as a desktop pattern. This is only visible when you're in that editor, but it gives you a good idea of what your pattern will look like spread across your desktop (this works for any PAT, including PAT 17), even though PAT 17 is the scroll bar pattern.

So now go ahead and make the pattern look however you want. When you're done editing the scroll bars and desktop (PAT #16), replace your old System with the new System and restart your Mac. You will get the patterns you created.

The PAT# editor

Now that you have learned how to make custom desk-top patterns, you may want to know how to save a bunch of them and then access them from the General control panel. To do this, you need to use the PAT# editor, since the PAT# is the resource where the system stores its built-in patterns. Open up the PAT# resource within the System, and open up resource number 0. If you get a dialog saying that the resource is compressed, go ahead and click OK. What this is telling you is that the System normally keeps this resource compressed, and if you make any changes, it will stay decompressed. There's no way around this except to not make changes, and then what's the point?

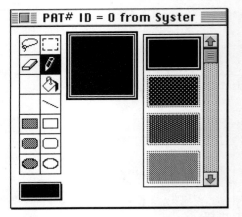

Figure 2 -

The PAT# editor showing PAT# ID 0.

The PAT# editor is very similar to the PAT editor, with one difference. The PAT# resource is a set of patterns, as opposed to the PAT, which is a single pattern. As a result, the area on the right contains all the patterns within the PAT# resource. To edit one, click on the pattern in the list on the right. That item will be selected, and the 8x8 pattern will show up in the middle. If you want to add your own desktop pattern, choose Insert New Pattern from the Resource menu. This brings up a blank pattern which you can change to suit your taste. As with all the pattern resources, you can go to the menu (named after whichever resource you are currently editing) and choose Try Pattern to see how the pattern looks when it's actually on your desktop.

One other useful aspect of this resource is that you can actually edit the patterns *ResEdit* has stored in its pattern palette (available in all the bitmap editors). You can add patterns to this palette, but they will only show up in black &white resources (excluding ICN#s and ics#s). All color editors have a fixed palette size, and you can only replace the existing patterns.

ppt#s

People with color Macs don't get black & white patterns in their General control panel. However, they do have access to some color patterns which are built in to the System. These patterns are stored in a resource similar to the PAT# resource, the ppt# resource. Go ahead and open up that resource.

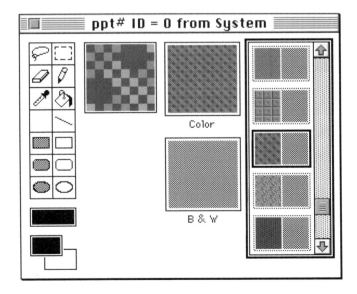

Figure 3 -
The ppt# editor.

If you took the time to look at the PAT# editor, you'll notice that the two editors are very similar. However, the ppt# editor has one important difference. The ppt# re-

87

source contains black and white information as well as color information. That way, you can modify a color pattern so that it still looks okay when you're running in black & white mode (of course, no black & white pattern can look as good as a color pattern!).

When you select a pattern from the list of ppt#s, it puts up the editing window for that pattern. Next to it, the editor puts a panel showing what the color pattern looks like, and below that it places a panel showing the black & white pattern. To the far right, you can see both the color and black & white variations of all the patterns in that resource. Select one of these to go to a new pattern. To make a black and white pattern from a color pattern (or vice versa), click and drag from one area to the other.

Editing color patterns is much the same as editing black & white patterns, except for the fact that *ResEdit* adds a color palette and an eyedropper tool.

As with the PAT# resource, you can insert a new pattern by choosing Insert New Pattern from the Resource menu.

That's all there is to editing the built-in patterns in the System. Go ahead and make some cool patterns and install your new System. That way, you can always switch between these patterns by going to the General control panel.

So far, except for editing the scroll bars, there's not much you can do to these patterns with *ResEdit* that you can't do with system software. For instance, under System 7, you can save your custom patterns (color or black & white) directly from the General control panel by double-clicking on the panel which shows what the pattern looks like in actual size (not the editing window). However, under System 6, you would need to use the *ResEdit* approach. The next section will show you how to make really big color patterns for your desktop.

ppats

Just as there is a color equivalent to the PAT# resource, there is a color equivalent to the PAT resource—the ppat resource. This resource tells the System what the current desktop pattern is (unfortunately, you can't make color scroll bar patterns with this resource). While it works much like the PAT editor, it has some important differences.

Again, open up a copy of your System file and open up ppat #16 (if you don't have one, use the Create New Resource and the Get Resource Info menu items to make one). This is the desktop pattern. You'll probably notice that it looks much like the ppt# editor, except that it doesn't have the long list of all the patterns in the resource.

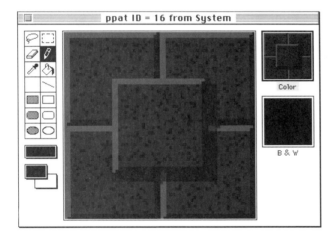

Figure 4-
The ppat editor.

To the left, you'll see all the common paint tools that you can work with. In the middle area you'll see the editing window for the pattern, and the representations of that pattern in color and black & white.

The really cool aspect of the ppat resource is that, on 32-bit QuickDraw machines (Mac IIs, LCs, Quadras, SE/30s, and Powerbook 140s & 170s) it can be made even bigger than the 8x8 standard. This way, if you find that small patterns annoy you (as they do me), you can make a substantially larger pattern. To do this, choose Pattern Size... from the ppat menu. You'll then get a dialog box like the one in Figure 5. To change the size, just click on the box which represents the dimensions you want, and click OK (or double-click on the box you want to use). The editor will then adjust its size to fit the new pattern.

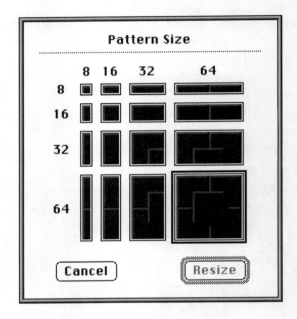

Figure 5 -
The ppat resize dialog.

One thing you may want to do when designing large patterns is to turn off the little grid lines that appear between the blown-up pixels. To do this, choose Visible Gridlines from the Transform menu. When this is unchecked, the gridlines will not appear, making it easier to work with the pattern. As always, you can choose Try Pattern from the ppat menu to see how the pattern looks on the desktop.

Although *ResEdit* can only work with patterns as big as 64x64, the System can actually handle any pattern whose dimensions are a power of 2. Thus, you could have a 1024x1024 pattern that filled your entire screen without repeating. However, since you can't do this with *ResEdit*, how would you do it?

Well, there are a few utilites which will allow you to do this. One of the best, though it's commercial, is *Wallpaper*, from Thought I Could! Software. It's a handy little cdev which makes editing big patterns really easy. Under System 7, *Wallpaper* files can be dragged and dropped into the System Folder to be installed into the System. It can even store them. In short, it's well worth the small amount of money it costs. There is also a shareware program called *DeskPat*, available from BMUG and other user groups and online services, which turns whatever is on the Clipboard into a ppat. Finally, another shareware program called *Desktop Pattern* will allow you to edit large patterns.

Since *ResEdit* can only recognize patterns of up to 64x64 pixels, you can only open ppats that are this big or smaller. If you try and open a larger ppat, *ResEdit* tells you that the resource is corrupted. That's only because it doesn't know how to deal with it. You can still move the ppat into the System and change the ID number; you just can't edit the resource.

There is one small problem with having ppats larger than 8x8: Once you install one, your General control panel will no longer show you color patterns or even let you work in color. So, if you decide to make a large desktop pattern, you've got to use *ResEdit* to work with your pattern. If you re-install the System, you will regain this ability. More importantly, if you go to the General control panel and choose the black & white pattern, you get that pattern, but you lose the ability to display a color pattern even if one is in the System. This includes the color controls in the General control panel. If this happens, your only option (unless you're using Wallpaper or something similar) is to re-install your System.

Now that you know all this, you can go on to make your own cool desktop patterns. If you make one you're really proud of, you may want to consider posting it to online services so that others can enjoy them.

Thanks to Andrew Wynn for his information about using ppats bigger than 64x64. He can be reached at Mac God on America Online.

Chapter Nine

Everything You've Always Wanted to Know About Fonts*

by Jens Peter Alfke

> Last year a lovely Berkeley Oldstyle Book,
> This year among the characters of Stone,
> All's the same to me:
> Clapping hands, the peaks roar at the blue!

*But Were Afraid to Ask

Everything you've always wanted to know about fonts

The Macintosh font system is a fine example of the phenomenon called thin ice. The friendly surface world of fonts, with its little pictures of suitcases and jolly names like StoneSerBolIta, is rather fragile. Poking too hard at it, putting too much weight on it, or just stepping in the wrong place, can send you crashing down into the depths; and the depths are much more complicated than the surface.

In the olden days of computers, rescue from below the ice was effected by shambling, superhuman programmers, who would stare at hex dumps, quaff mightily from tankards of cola, and patch your operating system until it spat you back out onto the surface. Today, in the have-a-nice-day world of the Mac, we have friendly programs with jack-in-the-box icons that give the same powers to non-programmers. At the risk of placing a dangerous amount of weight on my thin-ice metaphor, this article explains how to use a saw, wet-suit and scuba gear. It also describes some of the murky terrain of the riverbed. It is not a travelogue of the happy surface world; there are many good books and magazine articles that provide that. Let's dive!

Macintosh fonts (see below for information about PostScript fonts) are divided into four main types of resources. Each one is discussed briefly below.

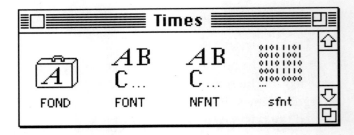

Figure 1 –
The different font resources.

FONT

ID	Size	Name
2560	0	Font Family: Times
2574	44	Times 14
2578	44	Times 18

FONTs from Times family

Figure 2 –

Fonts from the Times family.

Sensibly named, the FONT resource was the original font system introduced with the 128K Macintosh. With this resource, each size of font is stored in a different resource. Thus, Times 18 and Times 14 were two separate FONT resources. In this system, every typeface also includes a special FONT resource, which serves as a divider. It has no size, but its name is the name of the font. Thus, when you open a FONT resource, you'll see several resources which take up no space. This particular resource is used to store the name of the typeface. These resource names are the ones which actually end up being displayed in an application's font menus. All the Macintosh System fonts are still done this way up through System 6.0.7, though this changes with System 7, whose standard fonts do not use FONT resources.

FOND

Once the LaserWriter came on the scene and users started trying to produce real typography on the desktop, some substantial limits with FONTs became apparent. One of these limitations arose from the fact that there is no provision for typeface families, with true bolds and italics and the like. If you italicized some Times text, all that happened on the screen was that the Macintosh slanted the regular Times. If you emboldened it, the Macintosh smeared the original to make it darker. If you want to do real typography, these tricks just don't work. In addition to this, the widths of characters in a FONT are specified in points (or pixels), so every character had to be an integral number of pixels wide. However, real characters don't have such even widths, so round-off error was inevitable. This translated into badly-spaced text, since the Mac's and the LaserWriter's ideas of line widths came out different. (You will still run into this problem if you don't turn on your word processor's "Fractional Widths" setting.)

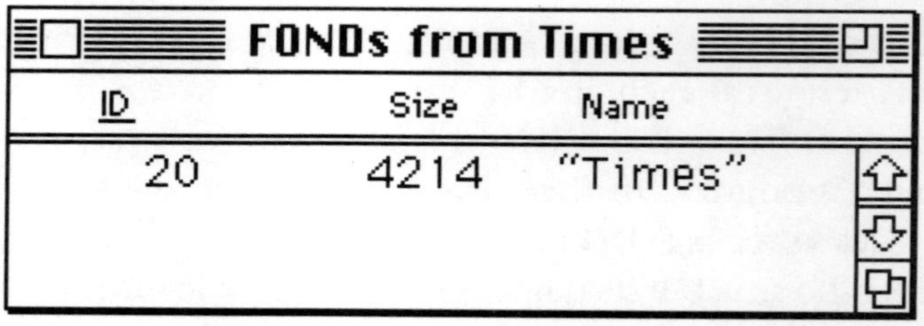

Figure 3 –
The FOND picker.

ID	Size	Name
20	4214	"Times"

FONDs from Times

The solution was a new resource to contain the extra information needed: the FOND, for FONt Definition. There is one FOND resource for each typeface. Its resource ID is the same as the font ID, and its name is the name of the typeface. The information in the FOND includes:

- High-resolution equivalents of values previously stored in FONT resources, such as the font ascent, descent and line spacing, and character widths. These are fractional values that can be scaled to any point size.

- Flags related to PostScript printing. These mostly tell what to do if some styles, such as a true bold or italic, are missing.

- A Font Association Table (FAT), which lists the resource IDs of FONTs (and NFNTs) to use for various point sizes and styles (see below).

96

```
▤▢▤▤▤▤▤  FOND "Times" ID = 20 from Times  ▤▤▤
  1) *****
  Font Size      │ 14   │
  Font Style     │ 0    │
  Res ID         │ 8010 │
  2) *****
  Font Size      │ 18   │
  Font Style     │ 0    │
  Res ID         │ 3314 │
```

Figure 4 –
The Times Font Allocation Table (FAT).

- A style table, which lists the PostScript font names to use for different styles. This is how the Mac tells the LaserWriter what fonts to use, and how it finds downloadable PostScript font files to send to the LaserWriter.

- Kerning tables for one or more styles.

NFNT

Even using FONDs, the font system was still limited as long as FONTs were used. Because of their strange numbering scheme, there was still only a tiny range of font IDs: from 0 to 255. This meant, of course, that no one could have more than 256 typefaces, including the ubiquitous Chicago and Geneva, installed at a time. If there were more than 256 Macintosh typefaces, some of them would inevitably have the same IDs. This limit was quickly reached, even before PostScript typefaces be-

```
▤▢▤▤▤▤  NFNTs from Times  ▤▤▤▤
   ID          Size       Name
  5674        3086       "Times"
```

Figure 5 –
The NFNT picker.

came widely available. *Font/DA Mover* tries to help. If you copy a new font into your System file, but the System already contains a different font with the same ID number, the incoming font will be renumbered as it's installed. This results in different sets of ID numbers on different Macs, the inevitable result being that your co-worker's document, set in New York, would appear in (yow!) Cairo on your Mac.

The obvious solution to this numbering problem was to fix the entire numbering scheme. This required using a new resource type (to avoid numbering conflicts with FONTs) even though the data inside stayed the same. Thus the NFNT, for New FoNT, or New Font Numbering Table, was born. NFNTs contain the same data as FONTs, but since they are referenced only through Font Association Tables (FATs), they can have arbitrary resource IDs. When copying fonts, the *Font/DA Mover* will renumber individual NFNT resources (updating the FAT references) to make sure that no two in the same file have the same ID. This renumbering causes no harm to documents, since NFNT IDs are normally used only by the internals of the Font Manager.

Freed of the 256-font limit, typefaces can have font IDs up to 16,383—as long as the bitmap fonts are contained in NFNT resources. (The range from 16,384 to 32,767 is reserved by the Script Manager for fonts of other writing systems such as Hebrew or Kanji.) Apple registered font IDs, making sure that no two fonts, even from different vendors, had the same ID. Everything seemed fine until mid-1990, when it came to pass that the entire range was used up. Now we're back in the same boat: there will be different fonts with the same IDs, and as a result, different people's systems may have different IDs for the same fonts.

sfnt

ID	Size	Name
3314	62212	"Times Bold"
6466	65408	"Times Italic"
6966	64276	"Times Bold Italic"
8010	63976	"Times"

sfnts from Times

Figure 6 –
The sfnt picker.

The sfnt is the latest addition to the family. sfnts are outline fonts, like PostScript fonts. This means that they contain mathematical descriptions (known as spline curves) of the outlines of characters. Apple's TrueType technology (built into System 7, and available as an INIT for System 6.0.7) can scale these outlines up to any point size and fill them in with pixels, allowing for smooth, well-shaped characters at large point sizes. This is a skill which bitmap fonts, such as those controlled by the FONT resource, sorely lack, as anyone knows who's tried to type in a size which is not available. TrueType and sfnt resources provide the same immediate advantages as *Adobe Type Manager.* However, sfnts are better integrated into the operating system, making them easier to install and more amenable to future growth. No separate downloadable PostScript font is required; the sfnt resource lives in a suitcase file or the System file, just as other font resources do.

What's in a font

A font, or typeface (the two terms have become almost interchangeable), is a set of images of characters. Since the characters are intended to be placed next to one another in a line, the resource includes not only the shape of each character, but its vertical alignment relative to the baseline and horizontal spacing relative to adjacent characters. (The alignment and spacing are called *metrics.*)

99

Sidebearings

Ascender

Baseline

Descender

Figure 7 –
Alignment and spacing
font metrics.

There is also information that applies globally to all
the characters, such as the leading — the distance between lines of type in a font. Technically, leading is the
amount of extra space between lines plus the point size,
measured from the baseline of one line to the baseline of
the next line. For example, 12 pt. type with a 14 pt. space
between lines (often called 12/14) has 2 pts. of leading.

Also, a font may have a table of kern pairs, which are
adjustments to the spacing between specific pairs of
characters, such as "A" and "V."

And, of course, every font or typeface has a name.

Beyond these attributes, there is also an internal set of
linkages that connect fonts to one another. In the old days
of just the FONT resource, there had to be a linkage
between different sizes and styles of the same typeface.
When you change text to 18 pt. Times Bold, the Font
Manager within the Macintosh can follow these linkages
to find the appropriate set of bitmaps, or the appropriate
TrueType outline, to display.

Editing font resources

ResEdit 2.1 provides a graphical editor for FONT and
NFNT resources, which lets you modify or create bitmap
fonts. It provides a textual, template-based editor for
FONDs, which lets you edit some parts of the FOND but

not others. It has no editor for sfnt resources, which are extremely complex in structure.

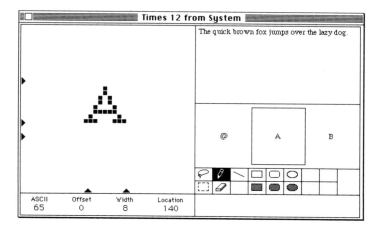

Figure 8 –
The FONT editor.

The FONT/NFNT editor

The FONT editor has several important components. As with all bitmap editors, the largest part of the editor is a FatBits view of the character you will be editing (in this case, the letter 'A' in Figure 4). To choose a different character, simply type it on your keyboard. The two upward-pointing triangles below the character mark the left and right sidebearings of the character—its left and right margins. Dragging these outward increases the amount of space around the character dragging them inward reduces it. It is perfectly all right for the character to stick out past the sidebearings on either side; this means that it will overhang neighboring characters. Many italic letters do this.

The baseline marker is the middle of the three triangles to the left of the character. It marks the baseline, the line on which all characters in a line, regardless of font, size or style, sit. It cannot be moved.

The ascender and descender lines are the other two triangles on the left side of the editing area (ascender is the top triangle) and mark the top and bottom of the entire font. No part of the font can go above the ascender or below the descender. (If you move these markers too far in, you will end up chopping off the tops or bottoms of letters. Be careful!) The ascender and descender are occasionally used to determine the line spacing of the font, but modern applications get this information from the FOND or make it up themselves.

Below the editing area are some numeric displays. These show more-or-less technical information that will probably not be of much use to the more casual user. The ASCII code is the internal code (0-255) of the character. The offset is the distance from the leftmost black pixel to the leftmost left-sidebearing marker of the entire font (sorry you asked?); the width is the set width of the character (the amount the "pen" moves when drawing that character, equal to the distance between the left and right sidebearing markers); and the location is the offset to the character's bitmap in the font's internal storage.

Finally, there is a sample text display at the top right, so you can see how the characters look in context. If your screen is not in color or grayscale mode, any changes you make to the characters will be reflected in the sample text. You can edit the sample text by clicking on it; then you can type, or drag to select text, as in any other text field. Clicking outside the text box removes the selection or insertion point. From then on, typing will switch to the character you typed for editing.

The FOND editor

The FOND editor is textual and based on a template. It's of limited use: It doesn't let you edit the kerning or style-mapping tables, and if the resource is too large it will refuse to open it at all. Still, it's very useful to be able to edit the font ID and the Font Association Table (FAT). In working with the FOND editor, keep in mind that many numeric values are shown in hexadecimal (base 16.) These are the numbers that start with a "$" and may include as digits "A" through "F". You can enter new decimal values in these spaces; just make sure to delete the "$". Similarly, if you enter a new hexadecimal value, make sure you keep the "$" before the number.

Most of the fields should remain undisturbed, but some can be very useful. For instance, several fields allow you to set extra widths for different styles (bold, italic, etc.). The FOND resource also has fields which can be used to set global values for the ascender and descender of a typeface, no matter what the size. Near the end of the FOND resource (directly before the field labeled "The Tables"), one can find the Font Association Table—the FAT.

The FAT lists the resource IDs of screen fonts (FONTs, NFNTs, and even sfnts) to use for various point sizes and styles within a FOND. Thus, when the computer needs to display text in a particular font, size, and style (for instance, 12 pt. Times Italic), it looks to the FAT area of the appropriate FOND to find which FONT, NFNT, or sfnt to use for that size and style. By including style information, it makes it possible to have real screen fonts for italic and bold styles.

The FAT is a typical *ResEdit* list. Each entry in the list consists of a point size, a style code, and the resulting resource ID. The point size is the actual size of the font you are referring to. The style code is the result of adding together various style values:

0	plain	32	Condensed
1	**Bold**	64	Extended
2	*Italic*	256	4-color font
4	Underline	512	16-color font
8	Outline	768	256-color font
16	Shadow		

Following this formula, Bold Condensed style would be 1 (Bold) + 32 (Condensed) = 33. In practice, only the Bold and Italic bits, and sometimes Condensed and Extended, are used.

NFNTs are accessed through the FAT and can be given any resource IDs, so long as those IDs don't conflict with any other NFNTs. A FONT resource can't be given a different ID just because it's being referenced through a FAT. It must still use the 128*font ID + size formula. (For this reason a typeface that uses any FONT resources cannot have a font ID greater than 255.)

If you renumber FONT or NFNT resources associated with a font, you must update the entries in the FAT.

Figure 9 –
FAT for System font.

```
┌─────────────────────────────────────────────┐
│▤□▤▤▤▤▤  FOND "Chicago" ID = 0 from System ▤▤│⇧│
│                                              ├─┤
│  1) *****                                    │ │
│                                              │ │
│  Font Size    │12          │                 │ │
│                                              │ │
│  Font Style   │0           │                 │ │
│                                              │ │
│  Res ID       │12          │                 │ │
│                                              │ │
│  2) *****                                    │ │
│                                              ├─┤
│  The Tables  $│                           │  │⇩│
└─────────────────────────────────────────────┴─┘
```

It's critically important, if there's any data at all shown in the "The Tables" box that follows the FAT, that you don't insert or delete entries from the FAT list. Changing the size of the FAT will invalidate internal pointers in the FOND tables, which will destroy its data and cause horrific effects, including system crashes, any time the system tries to use that font.

It's also very important that the entries in the FAT remain sorted. The point sizes are listed in increasing order, and within a point size, the style codes are listed in increasing order. If you don't do this, you will seriously annoy the Font Manager, and it will return many kinds of wonderful system errors.

You can use the FAT to change your System font. If you open the FOND resource for Chicago in the System file, you will notice one field which lists the size as 12. This is Chicago 12, and this is what the System looks for when it wants to know what FONT to use. Normally, the corresponding ID number is 12, which is the Chicago 12 installed into the System and the ROMs. However, there's no reason why the ID number can't be the ID number of another FONT. Simply type in the new ID, having found it from the FONT resource, and keep the size as 12 (although your ID number can represent a font of any size, since each FONT represents a certain size). There are some problems with doing this, however. One comes from making the new font too big. The Macintosh is nice enough to resize your menu bar and menus as needed to accomodate the font which is used for the system font, but it will not resize the dialog boxes. As a result, you'll get a dialog box which is the same size, with all the same information, but in a much larger font.

Editing sfnts...not!

ResEdit doesn't provide a sfnt editor, and probably won't in the future. sfnts are extremely complicated beasts, and editing spline data requires very sophisticated graphical editors. The only practical way to work with sfnts is to buy a dedicated type design program like Altsys' Fontographer, Letraset's FontStudio, or Kingsley/ATF's ATF Type Designer. Techies who simply must know how the data is organized should contact APDA (the Apple Programmer and Developer Association) at (800) 282-2732 and order the TrueType Font Format Specification, part number M0825LL/A.

There is actually one useful thing you can do with an sfnt resource: You can see the author and copyright infor-mation for the font. If you open the resource, you'll get *ResEdit*'s generic hexadecimal editor. By scrolling through the data, you can find the author and copyright information. It's hard to miss; it's about the only human-readable data in the entire resource. Look in the text column on the right side of the editor. The text will usually be located near the beginning or the end of the data. This is handy if you've obtained an ostensibly public-domain or shareware TrueType font and you want to make sure it's not really a commercial font. (Some people have been converting commercial PostScript fonts to TrueType, using utilities like Metamorphosis or FontMonger. The resulting TrueType fonts are still commercial, and distributing them is software piracy.) If you look at a "shareware" sfnt and find a copyright notice that says, for example, "Copyright ©1988 Adobe Systems, Inc.", that's what's happened. Get rid of it and inform the person you got it from.

Renaming or renumbering a FOND

In all modern Macintoshes, it is the FOND resource which gives a typeface its name and font ID. (Some old suitcase files may contain raw FONTs without a FOND, but *Font/DA Mover* will add the necessary FOND when it copies those FONTs into another file.)

If you wish to rename the typeface, all you have to do is use the Get Resource Info... command to change the resource name of the corresponding FOND resource. Keep in mind that all applications that store font names in documents (such as *PageMaker*) will no longer recognize the font name in existing documents, and will probably change the type to Geneva or Courier.

To renumber a typeface, change the resource number of the FOND. Then open the FOND and change the "Family ID" field to the new number. (If all the bitmaps for the typeface are stored in NFNTs, Apple suggests you use a new font ID in the range 256-1023, since that range is reserved for renumbered typefaces.)

If some of the bitmaps for this typeface are stored in FONT resources, you'll have to renumber all the FONTs since their numbering is based on the font id. For each FONT, compute the new resource number based on the new font id. The formula for 'FONT' IDs is (128 * Font-ID) + Point Size. Renumber the FONT resource accordingly, and change the resource number stored in the FAT.

Renumbering incurs the same problem as renaming; applications that rely on font IDs will lose references to the font stored in existing documents.

For people who use *Microsoft Word*: Never renumber the Symbol font if you plan on using *Word*'s formula commands. *Word* assumes that the Symbol font's ID is 23 when it displays math characters in formulas. If this is no longer true, you will get garbage characters, most likely in Geneva, in your formulas.

Inside PostScript font files

StoneSerBolIta

BerkeOldStyMedIt

ClelaBorEigOhFiv

ChicaLasGra

Figure 10 –

PostScript font file icons from several vendors – Adobe, Bitstream, ATF and Casady & Greene.

Downloadable PostScript font files aren't usually very interesting or informative to look at, but I'll describe them here for the benefit of those of you who simply must know everything. These files are just containers for the PostScript code that makes up a downloadable font. When a document being printed to a PostScript printer makes use of a PostScript font that isn't already living inside the printer, the Mac looks (by name) for a downloadable file for that font. Then, it sends the enclosed PostScript code to the printer. The result is that the font is now living inside the printer and can be printed.

Those weird file names

The filenames of downloadable PostScript fonts are a great source of amusement to nearly everyone. They're also very important, as you will agree if you've ever renamed one and then tried to print with that font.

When the Mac looks for a downloadable file for a particular font, it looks for it by the name of the PostScript font. Unfortunately, Macintosh filenames can't be longer than 31 characters, and some PostScript font names can exceed that limit. So the name of the downloadable font file is compacted. It uses the first five letters of the first word of the font name and the first three letters of each following word. (This is called the 5-3-3 rule.) Thus, the PostScript font called "Stone Serif Bold Italic" resides in a downloadable file called "StoneSerBolIta".

What's inside

Downloadable files contain only a few resources. Most, such as the BNDL, FREF, and ICN#, are just there to give the file its icon in the Finder. All the PostScript code is contained in POST resources.

The POST resources start with number 501 and increase from there. Each resource contains a flag byte, another byte of filler, and then the data. (The template provided by *ResEdit* is wrong. When you open POST resources, use the Open Using Hex Editor command to open them. Then you'll just get a hex dump.)

If the flag byte is 1, the rest of the data is plain text. POST 501 is almost always of this variety. The following text is the PostScript font header, which contains some interesting stuff like the PostScript font name, the font type (1 or 3), and the copyright notice.

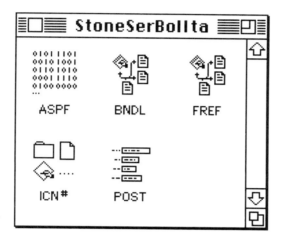

Figure 11 –

The resources within a PostScript font file.

Most of the succeeding resources have a flag byte of 2, which indicates compressed binary data. This is basically unintelligible to ugly bags of mostly water.

The last resource will have a flag of 5, which indicates the end of the data.

Some fonts have a POST resource with a flag of 3. This means that the rest of the PostScript data is in the data fork of the file, and isn't stored in resources at all.

Creating new FONTs

You can add new bitmap font sizes to simple type-faces that don't have PostScript fonts, kerning, or other tables. Before you start, open the typeface's FOND resource and check whether there's data in the "The Tables" box at the end of the display. If there is, you won't be able to add any bitmap fonts to this typeface—adding entries to the FAT would destroy those tables. If there's no data, it's safe to proceed.

To create a new size of an existing typeface, open up a suitcase containing all current sizes of that typeface with screen fonts stored as FONTs, not NFNTs. Open the FONT resource picker and use the **Create New Resource** command. Choose the appropriate typeface from the scrolling list, type in the point size, and press OK. A FONT editor will open for your new screen font.

Before you do anything else, drag the ascender up and the descender down enough to make room for drawing. Otherwise, nothing will show up. Then you can draw each character, making sure to move the sidebearings apart so the characters don't overlap.

Very important: After you're done, open the FOND and add a FAT entry for your new FONT. If you don't do this, the Font Manager won't find it.

Uses for bitmap fonts

There are still a few uses left for new all-bitmap typefaces. One use for the font resources is to add a character to a font. If you have a certain character which you would like to use, and it isn't in a font, you can just add it to the appropriate FONT resource (if the font is held in a FONT resource, like the Macintosh system fonts). Keep in mind that since each FONT represents one size, the special character will only be available in that size. To use it in all the sizes, you will have to add it to each separate FONT resource.

Another possible use for font resources is to add a new size to an existing font. This will take some time, but it can be worth it if a font you really like does not come in a desired size.

Jens Peter Alfke, after spending several years in the deserts of Arizona learning everything there is to know about fonts (and writing ATF Type Designer*), has returned to the fog-kissed Silicon Valley, where he now works on unspeakably cool projects for Apple Computer.*

Font overview

To get to the Font resources:

- Open *ResEdit*, and use it to open a program you wish to look at
- Double-click on the FONT, FOND, NFNT, or sfnt resource

To edit a FONT or NFNT:

- Double-click on the specific resource you wish to edit (e.g., FONT 12)
- Type the character you wish to edit to bring it into the display area
- Use the paint tools to edit the character

To add a FONT to a FOND resource:

- Double-click on the FOND resource you wish to add to
- Scroll to the area where your FONT will be added (remember that all fonts must be added in increasing order)
- Click on the row of asterisks prior to the next-highest size of FONT
- Choose Insert New Field from the Resource menu
- Enter the required information

Chapter Ten

Making Your Keyboard Work For You

by James W. Walker

Pounding on the keyboard,
thorns
sharp white.

Making your keyboard work for you

The following questions, posted by various users of CompuServe and UseNet, introduce some of the ways you might want to customize your keyboard.

Q: How do you keep the period and comma keys from changing with the Shift key, instead of turning into "<" and ">"? (The person who asked this question owns *Tempo II*, which didn't help and was also incompatible with *MacroMaker*. He could have bought *QuicKeys*, but of course that costs more money.)

Q: How do you exchange the functions of the Control and Shift keys?

Q: How do you remap the keyboard to the Dvorak configuration (a keyboard layout for English that is said to allow more efficient typing)?

Q: How do you make the Shift and Caps Lock keys cancel each other out? (That is, when you have the Caps Lock key down and you want to type an occasional lowercase letter, you might like the Shift key to switch you back into lowercase.)

Q: How do you disable the Caps Lock key? (Some people rarely use the Caps Lock key, but often hit it accidentally.)

All of these problems can be solved by using *ResEdit* to create or modify a keyboard mapping resource called the KCHR.

Each key on your keyboard, whether it's a character key or a modifier key such as Shift, has a numerical "raw key code." The operating system uses a table called a KMAP resource to translate the raw key code into a "virtual key code." For most keys, the virtual key code is the same as the raw key code. (When I simply say "key code," I mean virtual key code.) *ResEdit* does not have an editor for KMAPs, and I would not advise altering them.

For some international systems and some keyboards, the key codes are further rearranged using an "itlk" resource, but the U.S. system does not use an "itlk."

After a keystroke has been translated to virtual key codes, it is translated to a character using a KCHR resource. A KCHR resource contains several translation tables. Each combination of modifiers activates one of these tables, but a table may serve more than one combination of modifiers. Since there are five modifier keys (Shift, Option, Command, Control, and Caps Lock), there are 32 possible combinations of modifiers, so there could be up to 32 tables in a KCHR. However, the standard U.S. KCHR has only eight translation tables. For instance, translation table 0 is used for no modifier, or for Command, or for Command-Shift.

The author of this article has generously donated a file for the disk, called KCHR resources. *It contains many sample KCHRs you can paste into your own System and use.*

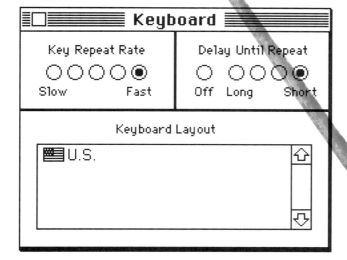

Figure 1 –
The Keyboard control panel, showing the list of available keyboard layouts.

If you have more than one KCHR installed in your System, you can use the Keyboard cdev (which comes with the system software) to choose between these different keyboard layouts (Figure 1). Note the small icon next to the keyboard layout in the bottom area of the window. I will discuss this later.

The KCHR editor

Figure 2 is a KCHR as displayed by *ResEdit*. At the time this screen shot was taken, the Command and Option keys were pressed. This caused those keys to be highlighted in the keyboard layout diagram at the bottom, and caused the appropriate translation table, Table 6, to be displayed.

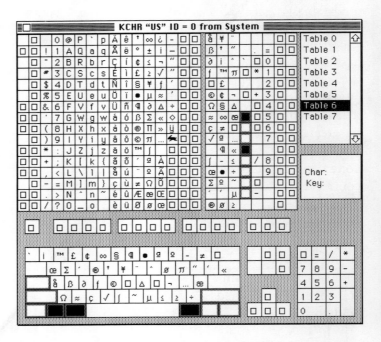

Figure 2 –
The KCHR editor.

In the upper left of the picture, there is a table of the ASCII character set, laid out in a 16x16 grid. This grid cannot be changed, except for the font and size. However, when you press a key, the character to which it is mapped will highlight in this grid. You can also drag characters from this grid to one of the other grids, as discussed later.

To the immediate right of the character array is a 16x8 array. The positions in this array represent key codes. The character at a given position is the one that corresponds to the key code, when a particular table is active. For instance, in the picture above, Table 6 has an infinity sign in the eighth row and second column in this smaller array. This means that the key code $17 (that's hexadecimal) gets translated to the infinity character when the Command and Option keys are pressed.

Remapping ordinary keys

Let's say we want to make Shift-period send a period instead of a greater-than sign. Find the period in the character array by pressing the period key. This will highlight the period key in the character array. Let go of the period key and press and hold the Shift key. Click the mouse on the period in the character array and drag it to the place you want it on the keyboard, i.e., right on top of the greater-than sign in the keyboard diagram. Release the mouse, then release the Shift key. That's it! What you've done here is hold down the Shift key to tell *ResEdit* that you wish to have access to the translation table corresponding to the Shift key. Then, when you move the period to its new location, you're making sure that a Shift-period will send this character. Note that when you let go of the Shift key (and return to the normal translation table), the period is still where it should be. This is because you have only modified the period key with the Shift key held down.

Remapping modifier keys

Recall that the various tables shown in the KCHR window correspond to certain combinations of modifier keys. The U.S. KCHR has eight tables. Experimentation reveals the correlation shown in Figure 3.

Let's suppose we want to exchange the roles of the Shift and Control keys. This will require a number of table reassignments. For instance, to assign Table 1 to the Control key, hold down the Control key and click on

117

Table	Modifiers
0	None, Command, Command-Shift, etc.
1	Shift
2	Caps Lock
3	Option
4	Shift-Option
5	Caps Lock-Option
6	Command-Option
7	Control, Control-Shift, Control-Option, etc.

Figure 3 –

A simple chart telling you which combinations of modifier keys belong to which tables in the U.S. KCHR resource.

Table 1 in the table list. *ResEdit* will show an alert asking if you really want to do this, as in Figure 4, below.

Figure 4 –

The Alert box asking you if you wish to replace the contents of a translation table.

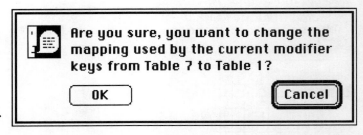

Click OK. You will also need to reassign Shift to Table 7, Control-Option to Table 4, Command-Control to Table 0, and so on.

I used this general technique to make the "No CapsLock" KCHR in *KCHR resources*. Since Figure 3 shows that two of the eight tables involve the Caps Lock key, I expected to be able to use the Remove Unused Tables menu command to get rid of two tables. That proved a bit tricky, because several modifier key combinations other than Caps Lock-Option were bound to Table 5. I had to uncouple the modifier keys (see below) and remove combinations like Caps Lock-Option-(right-hand Option).

Dead keys

In the standard U.S. keyboard layout, there are five keystrokes called "dead keys" that behave in a special way, in order to place accents on other letters. They are Option-e, Option-i, Option-u, Option-n, and Option-grave accent. For instance, if you press Option-e, nothing happens, so the key seems "dead"; but if you then press o, you get an accented o, ó. Only certain letters can take an accent. If you follow Option-e by a letter that can't be accented, like x, you get an accent followed by an x. Typing Option-e twice produces the accent alone.

If you type a dead key while in the KCHR editor in *ResEdit*, it brings up a special dead key editing window, depicted in Figure 5. You can also use the Edit Dead Key command from the KCHR menu.

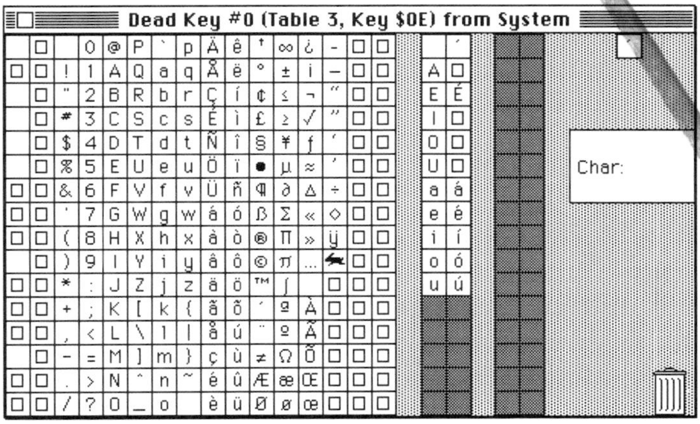

Figure 5 –
The dead key editor.

119

The biggest part of the dead key editing window is a character array, just like that in the main KCHR editing window. To the right of that, there is a list of pairs of characters. Each pair is simply the character, with and without the accent. The lone character near the upper right corner is the actual charcter and can be typed by typing the dead key twice or following the dead key by a character for which you have not defined an accent.

Now let's say you want to define an accented x to be an infinity sign, for some reason. Drag an x from the character array to the left-hand side of one of the unoccupied pairs, then drag an infinity character to the right-hand spot. If you change your mind, drag either of those characters from the pair list to the trash can.

To make the dead key into an ordinary key, just select **Remove Dead Key** from the KCHR menu.

KCHRs and the international Mac

Keyboard layouts are controlled by the part of the Macintosh system called the Script Manager. The Script Manager is responsible for the Mac's ability to work with different languages and writing systems. Each writing system, or "script," has an identification number. For instance, the Roman script, used for most European languages, is number 0, Japanese is 1, Arabic is 4, and Vietnamese is 30.

Each script has a range of possible KCHR ID numbers. The Roman script gets the lion's share of potential KCHR ID numbers, 0 through 16383. Each other script has a range of 512 KCHR numbers, starting from 16384 + 512*(script number - 1).

For each script, there is a currently active KCHR. The KCHR for the next time the system starts up is stored in an "itlb" resource whose resource ID is the script number.

The Roman script is always available. When another script is also available, the small icon representing the active keyboard layout will appear in the menu bar. You can switch scripts by clicking on this icon or by typing Command-space. There are also Command keystrokes that will simply set the script to Roman, or set it to the other script. (These keystrokes are specified in the "KSWP" resource.) To change keyboard layouts within a script, use Command-Option-Space.

Associating SICNs with KCHRs

Earlier, we discussed the fact that a KCHR could have a small icon (or SICN) associated with it. This is useful if you wish visual feedback about what keyboard layout you're using. If you are running System 6.0.5 or later, you can display the small icon of the current KCHR in the menu bar by modifying the itlc resource in the System file. Just set the "Always Show Icon" radio button to '1' or 'true.' This applies to System 7 as well as System 6. However, System 7 uses a new type of icon especially for keyboard layouts—the kcs resource. Unfortunately, *ResEdit* by itself does not allow editing of these icons. Fortunately, there is an editor from Apple employees available on most online services. Figure 6, below, shows what this kcs icon looks like for the U.S. keyboard layout. For more details about the menu under this icon, see below.

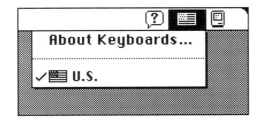

Figure 6 –

The small icon associated with the U.S. KCHR, shown in its position in the menu bar in System 7.

In order to create an SICN to attach to a KCHR, open the SICN resource in the System and choose Create New

121

Resource from the Resource menu. Edit the SICN until it looks the way you want. Now, give it the same ID number as the KCHR resource you want to attach it to. The System will associate the two resources.

Switching KCHRs without the Control Panel

ResEdit can be used to change which keys are used to activate an FKEY. Simply change the ID number of the FKEY to another single-digit numeral. This numeral is the new activation key.

I have included an FKEY called "switch KCHR" in the *KCHR resources* file. Once it is installed, you will be able to switch KCHRs by just pressing Command-Shift-7 rather than by using the Control Panel. Unlike the Keyboard cdev, switching KCHRs with the FKEY does not change the startup KCHR, only the active KCHR. This might be an advantage, especially if more than one person uses the same Mac.

There is another way to switch from keyboard layout to keyboard layout, without installing the FKEY. If you have set "Always Show Icon" to true in the itlc resource and you are running under System 7, you can click on the small icon in the menu bar to reveal a keyboard menu. With this menu, you can select all available keyboard layouts. For more information, you can choose About Keyboards…

If you are using System 6, but do not wish to install the FKEY, you may use a program called *Keyboard Switcher*, included on the disk which came with this book. This Control Panel device replaces the Keyboard Control Panel Device, and adds a menu which you can use to select various keyboard layouts. In addition to that, you may reposition the small icon associated with the keyboard.

Uncoupling modifier keys

You might wonder about the item Uncouple Modifier Keys in the KCHR menu. This option allows the right-hand

Shift, Option, and Control keys to be treated differently from their left-hand counterparts, at least on the Apple extended keyboard. Quoting *Inside Macintosh*, "This capability is included for compatibility with certain existing operating systems that distinguish the left and right keys. Its use by new applications violates Apple user interface guidelines and is strongly discouraged."

Some applications won't pay attention to KCHRs

Some applications may read the key codes, rather than the character codes, produced by the keyboard. Such keys cannot be remapped with a KCHR.

Other System 7 changes

In System 7, it is possible to install keyboard resources into the System by dragging a keyboard layout file to the System. The resource type of the small icons representing keyboard layouts changes from "SICN" to "kscn" and small icons will be available as KSC8's or KSC4's. Unfortunately, *ResEdit* does not have editors for these resources; however, kscn editors are available from BMUG and online services.

What can you do with this?

The KCHR resource can be used for a wide variety of purposes. As this article discusses, it can be used to set up keyboard layouts which may be more comfortable to you. For instance, if you are accustomed to the Shift and Control keys being in a different location (if you use another computer at home or work, for instance), you can simply swap them.

One common use of the KCHR resource is to swap the positions of the plus and minus keys on the numeric keypad. This is especially useful to people who use adding machines, and are used to the plus sign being below the minus sign.

Another potential use is if you have a special character (such as one produced by holding down the Option key) which you use frequently. By adjusting the KCHR, you can replace a character you rarely use with the character you often use.

KCHR overview

To get to the KCHR resource:

- Open *ResEdit* and use it to open the file you wish to look at (for KCHRs, this will generally be the System file)
- Double-click on the KCHR icon

To change one key to another:

- Find the key you wish to replace on the keyboard diagram
- Find the character you wish to replace it with on the character grid
- Drag the character from the character grid to the key on the keyboard diagram

To find a key on the character grid:

- Hold the key down on your keyboard
- The character will light up on the character grid and the keyboard diagram

To edit a dead key:

- Type the dead key (e.g., Option-e)
- Or, choose Edit Dead Key from the KCHR menu and select the dead key you wish to edit

James W. Walker is an associate professor of mathematics at the University of South Carolina, where he has taught since 1983. Jim can be reached on America Online as JWWalker, on CompuServe as 76367,2271, or on the InterNet as 76367.2271@CompuServe.com.

To attach a small icon to a keyboard layout:

- Under System 6, make an SICN with the same ID number as the keyboard layout
- Under System 7, use a third-party editor to make a kscn with the same ID number

To show the small icon associated with a KCHR:

- Open the itlc resource in the main window of the System file
- Set the "Always Show Icon" button to "1" (true) (System 6.0.5 or greater)

To remap a modifier key:

- In the KCHR editor, hold down the modifier key you wish to remap
- Click on the table you wish to remap it to

Chapter Eleven

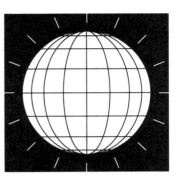

The International Mac

by Blaise R. Pabón

At last I've broken my country's barrier!
There are Macs everywhere – east, west; north, south.
On at morning, off at evening; neither host nor guest.
My every step calls up a little menu.

The international Mac

ResEdit has the power to modify programs to reflect differences in language and currency formats among users in foreign countries. Apple produces system software for many languages, and provides built-in support for "localization," or adapting software for different cultural conventions. This support exists in the form of the international utilities package.

The international utilities package makes use of several resources. In the beginning, there was one resource type called 'INTL' which contained two resources with IDs 0 and 1. INTL 0 contained the symbols for local currency, date, and time. INTL 1 contained the names of the months and the days of the week. INTL 1 also had a code which controlled alternative ordering sequences for sorting.

However, this created a problem when an application wished to suddenly switch to another local convention. As this was realized, Apple developed some new resources which were better equipped for switching quickly between different international setups. These new resource types were itl0 and itl1. At first, itl0 resources contained the same information, in the same format, as INTL 0, and itl1s contained the same information as INTL 1s.

By putting this information into separate resources, the Macintosh operating system could support multiple sets of local conventions. Any application may now switch date and currency formats within a single document.

ResEdit has complete editors for resource types INTL, itl0, and itl1. The editors within older versions of *ResEdit* were rather cryptic, but those included in this version of *ResEdit* are very straightforward. Like the other resource editors, they can be opened by double-clicking on the icon of the resource.

The itl0 editor

The itl0 editor allows you to edit both the INTL 0 resource and all resources of type itl0. The editor is broken into three main sections: Numbers, Short Date, and Time. Each one has several controls and fields which you can fill in to give you complete flexibility. When you alter one of the parameters in one of the sections, you get immediate visual feedback in the sample text in the lower left corner of each section. This is very useful for seeing how your changes look.

```
╔═▢════════════ itl0 "US" ID = 0 from System ══════════╗
║ Numbers:      Decimal Point: │.│      ⊠ Leading Currency Symbol ║
║         Thousands separator: │,│      ☐ Minus sign for negative  ║
║ ($1,234.50)   List separator: │;│     ⊠ Trailing decimal zeros    ║
║ ($0.5) ; ($0.5)    Currency: │$│      ⊠ Leading integer zero      ║
║ ........................................................ ║
║ Short Date:   Date separator: │/│     ☐ Leading 0 for day        ║
║              Date Order:│ M/D/Y ▼│    ☐ Leading 0 for month      ║
║ 4/3/91                                ☐ Include century           ║
║ ........................................................ ║
║ Time:         Time separator: │:│     ⊠ Leading 0 for seconds     ║
║ 11:44:53 AM  Morning trailer: │AM│    ⊠ Leading 0 for minutes     ║
║ 11:44:53 PM  Evening trailer: │PM│    ☐ Leading 0 for hours       ║
║             24-hour trailer: │     │  ⊠ 12-hour time cycle        ║
║ ........................................................ ║
║ Country:│ 00 - USA          ▼│ ☐ metric  Version: │1│ ║
╚══════════════════════════════════════════════════╝
```

Figure 1 –
The itl0 editor.

The "Numbers" section allows you to set the parameters for how numbers and currency are displayed. The four fields allow you to set the punctuation you wish to use as a decimal point, a thousands separator (as in 1,024), a list separator (when you have two values together), and a currency symbol. The check boxes on the right allow even more customization. "Leading Currency Symbol" determines whether or not the currency symbol is used at the beginning of the value or at the end. "Minus sign for

129

negative" allows you to choose whether or not the minus sign is used for negative numbers. "Trailing decimal zeros" gives you the ability to decide whether or not you wish to have two zeros appear after a decimal point. "Leading integer zeros," when set to true, places a zero before a decimal point if the value is less than one.

The "Short Date" section determines how the date will look when compressed into short date form (e.g., 12/7/70). With the pop-up menu, you can quickly switch between the six possible arrangements of year, month, and date in the short date. The "Date separator" field can be filled with the character or characters of your choice, and this punctuation mark will appear between all the values of the date. "Leading 0 for day" places a zero in front of the date if it is less than 10. Similarly, "Leading 0 for month" places a zero before the value for the month if it is before October (month number 10). "Include century" will force the entire year number to be placed in the short date (e.g., 1990 instead of 90).

The "Time" section has all the parameters needed for customizing the way in which time is displayed. As with the "Short Date" section, there is a field which lets you choose the character you want to use to separate the hour value from the minutes. With the three other fields, you can set the way the System indicates AM, PM, or Greenwich (24-hour) time. The check boxes are mostly for leading zeros (see above). The fourth check box, however, allows you to determine whether or not the default is 12-hour time.

Finally, there is a pop-up menu featuring the country codes, which lets you choose which country code is associated with your custom setup.

The itl1 editor

The itl1 resource contains the names of the months and the days of the week. These appear in boxes along the top half of the itl1 editor window. Across the middle of the window, there is a series of pop-up menus which allow you to change the sequence of day, month, date, and year. Between the pop-up menus are fields which can be used to indicate what sort of separators you want between all these values. In the lower left-hand corner, there is a sample of the date written with the current parameters.

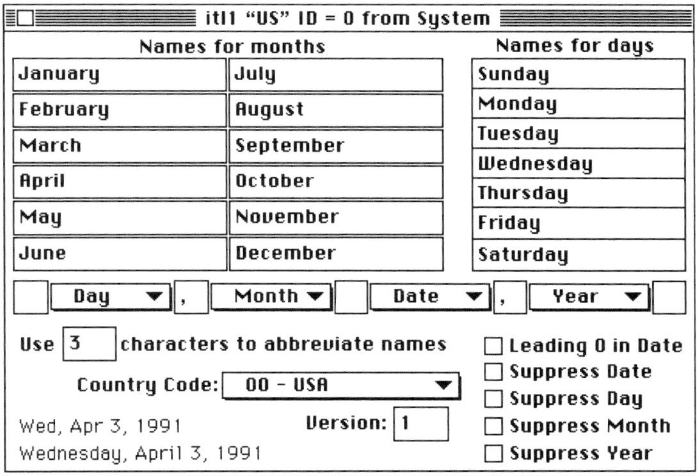

itl1 "US" ID = 0 from System		
Names for months		**Names for days**

Names for months		Names for days
January	July	Sunday
February	August	Monday
March	September	Tuesday
April	October	Wednesday
May	November	Thursday
June	December	Friday
		Saturday

Day ▼ , Month ▼ Date ▼ , Year ▼

Use `3` characters to abbreviate names

☐ Leading 0 in Date
☐ Suppress Date
Country Code: `00 – USA` ▼
☐ Suppress Day
Wed, Apr 3, 1991   Version: `1`
☐ Suppress Month
Wednesday, April 3, 1991
☐ Suppress Year

Figure 2 –
The itl1 editor.

As with the itl0 editor, you can select which country code you wish to associate with this resource. There is also a field which lets you specify how many characters are used when abbreviating a month or a day. The check boxes on the right side of the editor are mostly for suppressing values in the date. When one of these boxes is checked, or set to true, that value will not be shown in the date. The "Leading 0 in Date" places a zero in front of integers less than ten.

How this all works

In order to deal with foreign systems, Apple developed the Script Manager. The Script Manager is a collection of routines in the Macintosh Toolbox that provide support for non-Roman (other than American) writing systems. Arabic and KanjiTalk are two examples of conventions which are supported. Thus, applications which are Script Manager-compatible will accept non-Roman languages and print from right to left without modification. The Script Manager was implemented at about the time of System 4.1. After that, all Macs had the Script Manager built into their ROMs. This includes all Macs from the SE on up. The Script Manager is what uses the itl resources to adjust to international systems.

Normally, you will only require one set of local conventions, and since the same set of conventions can be shared by all the applications running under a particular system, the international resources are built into the System file. To determine which set of conventions will be used, the Mac OS searches for open resources, starting with the most recently opened resource. A document may contain a resource fork (*HyperCard* stacks, for instance), but since most do not, the most recently opened file containing a resource is usually the application, followed by the System file. If you want to ensure that a particular set of conventions is always available to users of your application, regardless of the current System, you should install the international resources into the application's resource fork.

Most current applications use the "new" resources (itl0, itl1, etc.), but some of the older ones may explicitly require the INTL resources. The System file also includes the INTLs for reverse compatibility, and you should keep in mind that you may need to customize the INTLs also. If you have carefully customized some local conventions only to find that an application requires them to be in the INTL 0 resource (or vice versa), open your new resource with Open Using Hex Editor under the Resource menu, select the entire contents, and copy it to the Clipboard. Then you can open the other resource type, create a new resource, open it using the hex editor, and paste.

What can you use this for?

These resources are used mostly by programmers, but the average user can also find many uses for the itl0 and itl1. For instance, a person might be used to working on a foreign Macintosh, and would be more accustomed to a different setup. To avoid confusion, they could reset these parameters to make the formats similar to what they are used to.

Another possible use is if a person is practicing a foreign language. With the itl1 resource, they can set all the values in a date to match the language they are studying.

If you frequently correspond with another country, you can temporarily reset the values for the parameters, and then all the numbers in your document will be in a format which the recipients will understand.

International overview

To get to the itl0 (currency, time, date) resource:

- Open *ResEdit* and use it to open a copy of the System
- Double-click on the itl0 resource

To get to the itl1 (month and date formats):

- Follow the same steps as above

Blaise Pabón is the Macintosh support specialist at Syntex Labs. He is the author of "PostScript Imprescindible," the first book in Spanish about the PostScript language.

Chapter Twelve

Dialog Boxes for the Non-Programmer

by Derrick Schneider

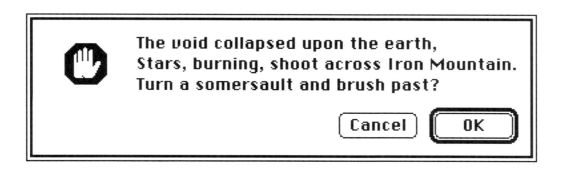

The void collapsed upon the earth,
Stars, burning, shoot across Iron Mountain.
Turn a somersault and brush past?

Cancel   OK

Dialog boxes for the non-programmer

Many Mac programs have certain common resources, simply because they are Macintosh applications. Menus and icons, covered in previous chapters, are two of these. Two other common types are dialog boxes and alert boxes. The best example of a dialog box is the one you get when you instruct an application to open a document. This is known as the "Standard File Open Dialog Box" (see Figure 1, below). Everyone who has tried to throw an

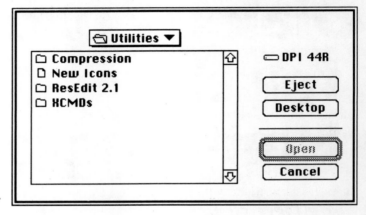

Figure 1 –

A Standard File Open Dialog Box under System 7.

application or System file into the Trash knows what an alert box is (see Figure 2, below). These are usually accompanied by a beep in order to attract your attention.

Figure 2 –

The Empty Trash alert box under System 7.

Dialog boxes and alert boxes both have certain standard components. Let's look at each of these items in more depth.

Push buttons are the rounded rectangles within a dialog box which usually contain the words like "OK" or "Cancel." They either are used to select a file or folder or dismiss the dialog or alert box.

Check boxes are usually used to indicate an option which can be toggled on and off. The user doesn't have to do anything with a check box; it can just sit there.

Radio buttons require a user to make a selection from a range of choices, each with its own radio button. The user does not have the option of leaving them all off or selecting more than one. With a group of radio buttons, only one may be selected at a time. If there are two or more groups of radio buttons, one in each group must be selected.

Control refers to the scroll bars used in a long list.

Static text is the text which is permanent for the dialog. Looking at Figure 2, the phrase "Are you sure you want to…" is static text. It can be changed in *ResEdit*, but it cannot be altered in any way within the dialog itself.

Editable text is the text which the user types into the dialog box. The most well-known example of this is in the "Save" dialog box of every Macintosh application. When you save a document the first time, you are asked to provide a name. The place where you type this name is an editable text field.

Icons are can be used in a dialog.

The **PICT** is the other type of graphic element. The major benefit of a PICT rather than an ICON is that a PICT is not limited to 32 by 32 pixels.

User Items are items which the programmer specifies. These are objects not supported separately by the Dialog Manager within the Toolbox. Some examples of User Items include pop-up menus, thermometers (which indicate progress of an action), and userText, which can be used to create different font styles within a dialog box. Since this item is for programmers, I will not discuss it here.

Editing the dialog

To get a practice dialog, open a copy of the Finder with *ResEdit*. Open the DITL resource within the Finder and choose Create New Resource... from the Resource menu. *ResEdit* gives you a blank dialog box with the DITL tool palette, which looks like Figure 3, below.

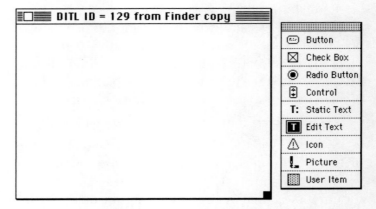

Figure 3 –
The DITL editor in *ResEdit*.

To add an item to a dialog box, click and drag the desired tool from the tool palette. You may wish to experiment to see how items with odd sizes (such as really big buttons) are presented within the dialog. For now, create one of each item in your dialog box (except for User Items).

Right now, your dialog doesn't say much. Your check box has the words "Check Box" next to it, and your radio button has the words "Radio Button" next to it. Double-click on the "Check Box" item to edit it. You should get something which looks like Figure 4.

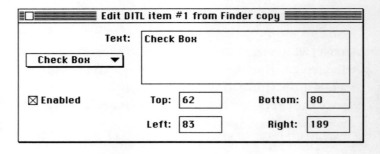

Figure 4 –
The DITL text item editor.

Let's look at each of these parts. There is a pop-up menu on the left which lets you change in an instant what kind of item it is. For instance, let's say that you had finished your dialog box, and then realized that you put a check box where you wanted a radio button. Just open the pop-up menu and choose Radio Button. Your item will suddenly be a radio button.

The title of this window indicates that this is DITL item #1. What does this mean? I'll discuss this in more depth later. For now, just realize that each item in a dialog has a number associated with it so that it can be called by the programmer.

The "Text:" box allows you to change the text which appears next to the item, if applicable. This applies to check boxes, radio buttons, static text, and editable text. In the first three, this text is permanent; it can't be changed except in *ResEdit*. In editable text fields, however, this is the default text of the field; it can be changed by the person using the application. For example, when you save an item and are asked what to name the file, most programs will already have a name in this field. You just type over it. The default text can be set here.

The "Enabled" check box below the pop-up menu allows you to determine whether or not an item is enabled. If this is not checked, the user will see a "grayed-out" button, check box, radio button, or text entry field, which cannot register mouse clicks or accept text.

The four fields below the "Text:" field tell you the dimensions of the item. "Top" and "Bottom" indicate what pixel rows the item spans. Similarly, "Left" and "Right" tell you which pixel columns the item's edges are on. Note that these are relative to the dialog box itself, not to the screen. Thus, in Figure 4, the top edge of the check box is 47 pixels from the top of the dialog box, and the left edge of the check box is 41 pixels from the left side of the dialog box. (The 0 position is defined as either the top-most row or the leftmost edge of the dialog).

Now, these windows can look a little bit different, depending on what item you have selected. In Figure 5, below, I have opened the item editor for my icon.

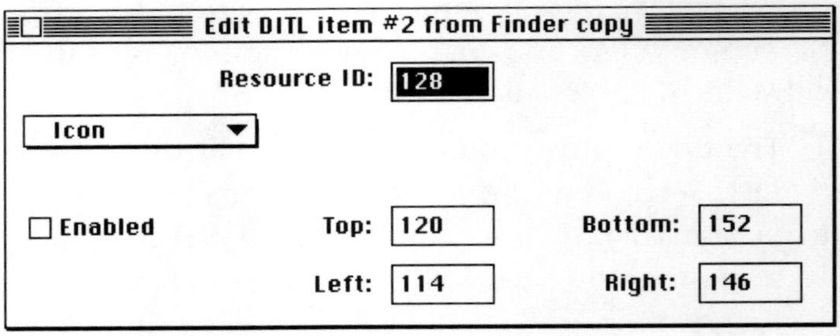

Figure 5 –
The DITL icon item editor.

This window is almost the same, but it has one important difference. In the check box item editor, we had a "Text:" field. In this editor, we can see that the field now says "Resource ID:" This editor allows you to set which icon you wish to use by its ID number. To use a new icon, simply type in its number. If you type in an ID number and that icon does not exist, *ResEdit* will show you a generic icon. However, your dialog will not work properly in the program.

Notice the "Enabled" check box again. You might be wondering how an icon can be "enabled" or "disabled." Well, programs can be told to look for the user clicking on the icon (or the picture, which has the same editor as this one). Some programmers might use this to bring up a short piece of info about themselves or the program.

DITL menu items

In the DITL menu, you can choose from a wide variety of commands to help you with your design. Some of these deal with item numbers, which are discussed in more depth below.

Renumber Items... allows you to quickly change the numbering of items. When you choose this menu item, simply hold down the Shift key as you click on the items in the order that you want them to appear. The first item you click on will always be given the new number 1 (the new numbers show up to the left of the old numbers, which are visible while this command is active), which can lead to trouble if you're not careful. If you want to change the positions of items 4 and 5, your first instinct would be to shift-click on item number 5 and then item number 4. However, this would cause item number 5 to be renumbered to item number 1, and item number 4 to be renumbered to item number 2, and the original item number 1 and item number 2 would then be renumbered. Therefore, you must shift-click on the original item number 1, then item number 2, then item number 3, and then you can rearrange items 4 and 5. (You may need to play with this to get a feel for it.) You may prefer, in this case, to use the menu command Set Item Number to give this item a new number. Note, however, that other items will be renumbered, so you may wish to do this with caution.

The Select Item... command allows you to select an item by its number. Once you type in the number, the corresponding item will become selected, and you can manipulate it.

The Show Item Numbers command will, when checked, show all the item numbers of the items in your dialog. The number appears in the upper right corner of each item. This way, you can quickly see which item is which.

The Align to Grid command constrains your items to an invisible grid. This way, the items can only be put on the grid, aligned to one of the lines.

The Grid Settings... command allows you to choose the spacing of the grid.

The Show All Items option forces *ResEdit* to put a rectangle around all the items in the dialog box. This rectangle is the rectangle which is defined in the item editor (pixels from the top, etc.).

The View As... command allows you to look at the item in a different font. However, this will not show up in the actual dialog box; it is only for your convenience. Dialog boxes are set at Chicago 12, by default. Except with User Items, this is not changeable in a specific DITL resource.

ResEdit 2.1 is set up so that people can begin publishing software for System 7. One of the best examples of this is the Balloon Help... menu command. This allows you to select which "Help balloon resource" you wish to use. System 7 features the capacity to have help balloons in dialog boxes. Thus, a person who is unsure of what a dialog box item does could click on a help balloon to gain some more insight about it.

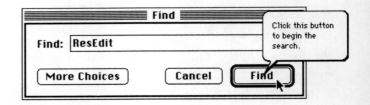

Figure 6 –

An example of *System 7's* Balloon Help.

The Alignment menu is fairly self-explanatory; it allows items in a dialog box to be lined up with one another. In order to use this, two or more items must be selected. Select more than one item by holding down the Shift key while clicking on each item.

The DLOG and ALRT resources

DITLs only control what appears in a dialog box. Two other resources, DLOG and ALRT, determine whether the dialog box is a regular dialog or an alert.

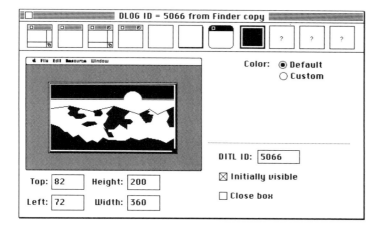

Figure 7 –

The DLOG editor, opened for a resource in the Finder.

The most prominent aspect of the DLOG editor is a miniature version of the Macintosh screen (complete with desktop pattern). This allows you to position your dialog box on the screen. To move it, simply click and drag it to its new location.

Another important aspect of the DLOG editor is the row of window styles along the top of the screen. Let's look at these one by one. The first from the left is a standard window, complete with scroll bars and a grow box, but missing a zoom box in the upper right corner. The next one is a window with just the close box in the upper left corner. The third is a normal window, with a title bar, close box, zoom box, grow box, and scroll bars. Next is a window with a title bar, close box, and zoom box, but missing everything else. Next is just a plain rectangle. Similar to that is the rectangle with a drop shadow, which can add a little bit of depth to your image. Although it is hard to see due to the fact that it is highlighted in my example, the next style is a rectangle with a double border around it. This is a common style for alert boxes. The last three styles can be defined by you, if you have developed a custom WDEF (Window DEFinition) resource, or if you have one you would like to use.

At the bottom left corner of the DLOG editor, you can see the measurements (in pixels) of the dialog. As before, 0 is defined as either the top of the screen or the left edge, depending on context. When you have a DLOG, you must tell the Macintosh which DITL resource it is controlling. This is the purpose of the "DITL ID:" field. If you double-click on the sample dialog box on the miniature Macintosh screen, you will bring up the DITL editor for that resource. There is also an option for determining whether or not a dialog is visible as soon as it is called. The final item is the check box for the close box. If this is selected, the window will have a close box in the title bar. If not, the window won't have a close box.

Finally, there is the ALRT resource. This is actually very similar to the DLOG editor, with some slight differences. Again, it allows you to reposition the dialog box and determine its size. It does not have the option of different window styles, nor does it have the "Initially visible" or "Close box" options. It does still have a field containing the ID number of the DITL resource you will be using.

In summary, DITLs are the resources which control what items are in a dialog. DLOG and ALRT then determine where the DITL is and what kind of dialog it is: regular or alert.

Numbering

Remember I said earlier that all items in a dialog have a number associated with them? This is very important. If a user clicks on an item, how does that cause resource information to be fed to the program? The answer is through the numbers. By using the item numbers, a programmmer can tell a program to do one thing if a radio button is "true" (selected) and another if it is "false" (not selected). The programmer does not type in "Tell me what that radio button says." He or she types in "Get the return from item number 6." The program does not know that it is looking at a radio button; it only tells itself that the result is "true" or "false." Thus, numbering is very important. When a resource is activated, all the items send info to the program, and it is up to the programmer to work with that. Even items which are not selected send back "false" messages, so that the program knows that that option was not selected.

Items can send back other information as well. Editable text sends back the contents of the field. Static text sends back what it says, even though this doesn't change while the dialog box is active.

Certain items have special requirements for numbering. One of these is the default button. Dialog boxes often have a default button (indicated by a thick, black border) which you can usually hit <Return> to activate. This button is item number 1. It is always a good idea to have item number 1 be a button. This prevents confusing results. Similarly, item number 2 should be another button (usually "Cancel"). This can be different for alerts, but it is not advised.

Another important concept in numbering is with radio buttons. You may have noticed that, when you have a group of radio buttons in a dialog, you can only select one of these. This is due to the numbering of this group of radio buttons.

145

When you assign numbers to them, you must make all the radio buttons in a group sequential and consecutive. In other words, the radio buttons, in order to work properly, must be items 3, 4, and 5. They cannot be 3, 6, and 8, because then they will all be considered to be separate groups. The Macintosh's Dialog Manager then makes sure that one is selected at a time. If you have two groups, they must be separated by at least one other dialog item.

Color dialogs

People with color Macs will see a slightly different DLOG and ALRT editor. With color capability, a pair of radio buttons will be visible. These let you choose between the default colors and a custom set of colors. To add your own color scheme, choose the "Custom" radio button. *ResEdit* then presents you with color palettes for a wide variety of the areas in the dialog which are fairly self-explanatory—"Frame" is the frame of the dialog; "Content" is the main area in the dialog; etc.

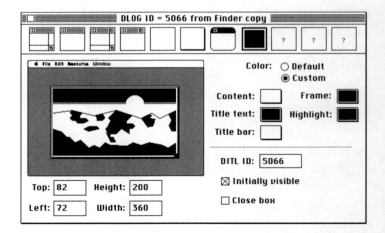

Figure 8 –
The color DLOG editor.

To choose a new color, click and hold on one of these boxes and a palette of colors will appear. Still holding down the mouse button, move to the color you wish to use.

When you add colors, *ResEdit* will warn you that it is about to add a new dctb. This is short for Dialog Color TaBle, and it represents the colors in a DLOG. The dctb will have the same resource ID number as the DLOG it is used for.

This same technique can be used for alerts as well, but *ResEdit* will add an actb to the file instead of a dctb.

Other stuff

As you are going through dialog boxes looking at the various designs, you may notice some which contain characters such as "^0" or "^1" or something similar. These are placeholders for the programmer. When the programmer writes the command which calls up the dialog box, he or she can change the placeholders into static text. While the static text will not change within one dialog box, it can be modified each time the dialog is brought up. Again, look at Figure 2, the alert box which appears when you empty the trash under System 7. If you look at this alert box with *ResEdit*, you will see a placeholder. This way, the programmer can get the size of the item you're tossing out, and then stick it into that placeholder.

Most of the time, these placeholders get information from the STR# resource within a program. The STR# resource, however, is capable of much more. For instance, open STR# resource #128 in the Finder (Figure 9, below).

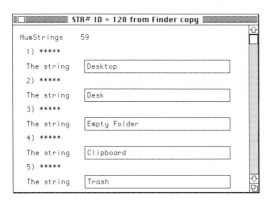

Figure 9 –

The STR# Resource from the Finder.

If you look at some of these names, they will no doubt ring a bell—for instance, the word "Trash" in the bottom text field. This is the string which the Finder puts under the Trash can. Thus, if you make your Trash can into something different, you may wish to change this string so that it is still relevant to your new icon. (For more information about editing icons, see the Chapter 4, "I think ICON.") Also, you will see that, in Figure 7, the word "Desktop" is highlighted. With this, you can change the name of the Desktop file. **This is not advised, as it can lead to severe errors. Never modify the Desktop except to rebuild it!** The word "Untitled" is the default name of a newly initialized disk. If you always name your new disks "Blank," you can make that the default with this resource. The word "Empty Folder" is the default name of a newly made folder. This can be easily changed to "New Folder" or something similar. To make changes to an STR# resource, simply edit the text as you would in any word processor.

Most people who create dialogs are programmers. However, there is nothing to stop you from editing dialogs in existing programs. Some people alter dialog boxes so that the contents say something different. Others like to put in new items which have no meaning at all, as practical jokes. However, you should always be careful about editing dialogs. Never change an existing item into another type, or rearrange the numbering scheme. The program will probably get very confused if you change a radio button into a check box. With this tip in mind, you should be fairly safe.

Thanks to Terry Teague from Apple Computer for his information about color dialogs. Terry Can be reached at TEAGUE.T on AppleLink.

Dialog box overview

To get to the dialog resources:

- Open *ResEdit* and use it to open the file you wish to look at
- Double-click on the DITL resource to show all the dialog item resources
- Double-click on the DLOG resource to show all the dialog resources
- Double-click on the ALRT resource to show all the alert resources

To change the text of an item:

- Double-click on an item within the DITL
- In the editor, type the new text into the "Text:" area

To change the icon or picture used in a dialog:

- Double-click on the ICON or PICT resource
- Type in the ID number of the resource you wish to use instead

To renumber the items in a dialog box:

- Choose Renumber Items... from the DITL menu
- Click on the items in the order (starting from 1) you wish to put them in

To choose a Balloon Help resource for a dialog:

- Choose Balloon Help... from the DITL menu
- Type in the number of the help balloon resource you would like to attach

Chapter Thirteen

Customizing Your ImageWriter

by Leonard Morgenstern

Black, Black, Black,
words splash
the snow-field.

Customizing Your Imagewriter

Are you irritated by the ImageWriter's printer driver and its five paper sizes, four of which you never use? Would you rather print 3x5 inch cards, or 9.5x6 inch notebook pages? Some word processors make it easy to print these odd sizes: for example, *Microsoft Word* has its Style Sheets. But if your communications program or spreadsheet lacks this flexibility, *ResEdit* provides you with a means to modify the PREC resources.

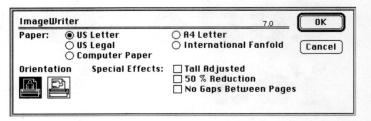

Figure 1 –
The ImageWriter page setup dialog.

First steps

Make a copy of your ImageWriter printer driver (in the System Folder). Move this to another disk or to another folder on your system disk. This will be the copy you work on. Use *ResEdit* to open this copy, and then open the PREC resource. You are interested in PREC ID 3. Double-click on this, and you should see the PREC editor, shown in Figure 2.

PREC ID = 3 from ImageWriter	
Number of Btns	5
Btn 1 Height	1320
Btn 1 Width	1020
Btn 2 Height	1400
Btn 2 Width	990
Btn 3 Height	1680
Btn 3 Width	1020
Btn 4 Height	1440
Btn 4 Width	990

Figure 2 –
Top o' the PREC.

The PREC editor

This editor is just a standard *ResEdit* list, such as we saw in the LAYO resource and the FOND resource. To edit a value, simply type over it, just as if you were in a word processor.

The first field in the editor, "Number of Btns" determines how many different page sizes will be given to radio buttons in the printer dialog. The default is five.

The next several fields are labeled, alternately, "Btn x height" and "Btn x width," where x represents any number between one and the number of radio buttons you have designated plus one. This is why these fields go from one to six, despite the fact that you only have five buttons. These fields control the heights and widths of the paper size. These are the juicy parts.

The numbers in each of these fields are given in 1/120th of an inch. To determine what size a piece of paper is, divide the values by 120. In the second field, then, we see that the height for "Btn 1" is 1320. If we divide this by 120, we get 11 inches. The width for "Btn 1" can be calculated the same way to yield 8.5 inches. We can now see that button one represents a standard sheet of paper. When you add your own values, you have to multiply the inch measurements by 120 to give you the proper point values for the PREC resource.

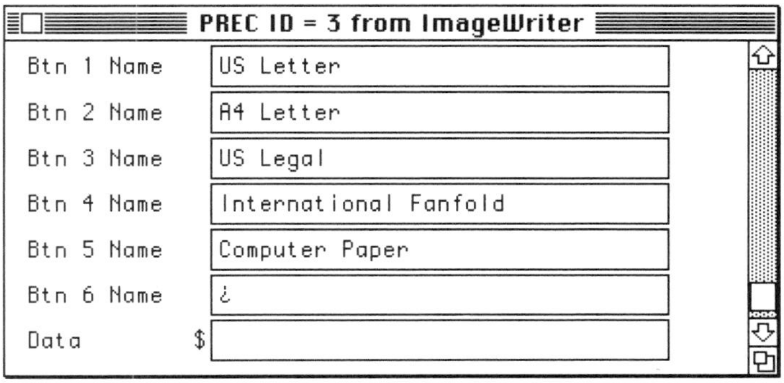

	PREC ID = 3 from ImageWriter
Btn 1 Name	US Letter
Btn 2 Name	A4 Letter
Btn 3 Name	US Legal
Btn 4 Name	International Fanfold
Btn 5 Name	Computer Paper
Btn 6 Name	¿
Data	$

Figure 3 –
Bottom o' the PREC.

If you scroll to the end of the PREC editor, you will see a set of fields labeled "Btn x Name," where x again represents any number between one and the number of buttons you have plus one (see Figure 3). By looking at them, we can see that these are the names of the buttons in the printer dialogs. In the field "Btn 1 Name," we see that the name of this button is "US Letter." The "Btn 6 Name" field does not have a name, but it does have a '¿' character. This character represents a placeholder. Since this field has to be filled, the programmer put a nonsense character into it. However, a program can use button six for a custom size by replacing this character.

The final field, "Data," should not be tampered with.

PREC 4 resources

Some programs have built-in printer drivers, which are designated PREC 4. You modify them the same way as you do PREC 3. They can be found in the PREC resource within an individual application.

Uses for the PREC resource

As mentioned earlier, the only reason for modifying the PREC resource would be to create custom paper sizes on a printer. Many people no longer use "real" computer paper (the really wide stuff with green and white bands), partly because the ImageWriter II cannot support paper this wide. However, many people might wish to print out their Rolodex cards, or a set of mailing labels. By altering the measurements associated with a button, you can set this up fairly quickly. You will have to play with the different printer drivers to see which PREC resources they use.

PREC overview

To get to the PREC resource for an ImageWriter:

- Open *ResEdit*, and use it to open the ImageWriter driver in your System Folder (Extensions folder under System 7)

To calculate the number of points from the number of inches:

- Determine the number of inches
- Multiply this number by 120

Chapter Fourteen

The Biography of a Program: vers

by Brian Novack

Were it not for
1.0
would the program be?

The biography of a program: vers

Certain aspects of the Macintosh user interface are always present from the moment your computer has finished its startup process until you shut the machine off. These include things like icons, the menu bar, and the trash can, to name a few. Usually, these features are enough to provide you with the information you need to use your favorite word processor, paint program, or communications program without any difficulty.

```
════════════════ HyperCard Info ════════════════

       📚  HyperCard

       Kind : application program
       Size : 674K on disk (689,157 bytes used)

      Where : DPI 44R : HyperCard folder :


    Created : Sun, Nov 11, 1990, 5:55 PM
   Modified : Wed, Apr 3, 1991, 1:50 PM
    Version : HyperCard 2.0v2
              ©1987-90 Apple Computer, Inc.
   Comments :
   ┌─────────────────────────────────────┐
   │                                     │
   │                                     │
   │                                     │
   └─────────────────────────────────────┘
                         ┌ Memory ──────────────┐
                         │ Suggested size: 1,000 K│
   ☐ Locked              │ Current size:  1000  K │
                         └────────────────────────┘
```

Figure 1 -
The Get Info...box

However, there comes a time when each of us needs just a little bit more information than these features provide. At this point, some of us will reach for the good old Get Info… menu item in the Finder's File menu to find out who wrote the software (so we can call them and beg for free upgrades), when it was written (so we know when it is time to call them for free upgrades), and which version of the software you have (so you don't beg for a free upgrade when you already have the current version and come away looking greedy).

The Get Info box has two parts:

- version information about the software, which is the area of our current concern

- a comment box

The comment box allows the user to type in a comment about the program or file. This information is then stored in an invisible file known as the Desktop file (one of those special files that we don't play with). This is why rebuilding the Desktop causes this information to be lost. The version information in the Get Info… box comes from the vers resource.

Using the vers editor

To look at the vers editor, open *ResEdit* and use it to open a copy of your favorite program (it must be an application or System file). Click twice on the vers icon.

The vers editor has six areas of information. Version number tells you what the version number is for this application (also seen in the Get Info… dialog box). The Release pop-up menu tells you what stage of development the product is in (see below). If the product is not actually released, there will be information in the non-release area which, together with the Release stage of development, will tell you how far along the non-release is. There is also a pop-up menu with all of the country codes in the

Macintosh System. This tells the Macintosh which international system should be used. The Short version string field will only contain the version number of the application. The Long version string field contains a more detailed description of the version information. All of these areas can be changed rapidly, either by typing in a new value or by choosing a new option from the pop-up menu.

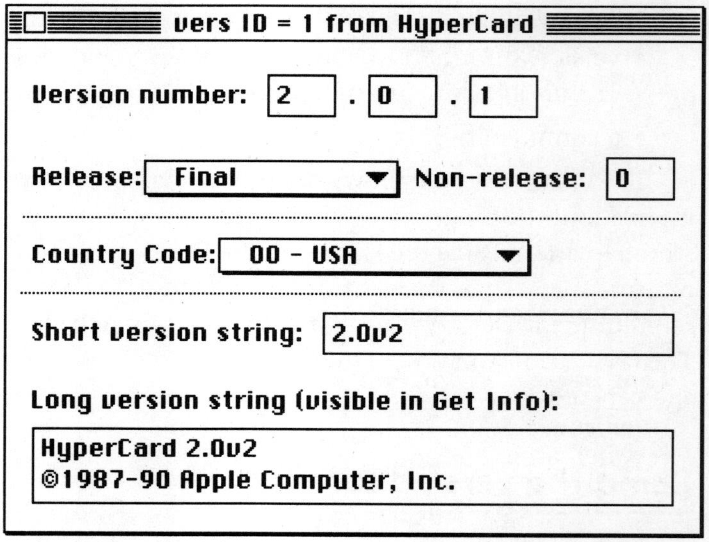

□ ▦▦▦ vers ID = 1 from HyperCard ▦▦▦

Version number: `2` . `0` . `1`

Release: `Final ▼` **Non-release:** `0`

Country Code: `00 – USA ▼`

Short version string: `2.0v2`

Long version string (visible in Get Info):

`HyperCard 2.0v2`
`©1987-90 Apple Computer, Inc.`

Figure 2 -
ResEdit's vers editor.

Apple has set forth specific guidelines on how to properly number the version information (Apple's Version Numbering Scheme). The first number is the release number (in our example, a 2), which can be any integer. This is followed by a period. Following this is a revision number (a 0 in our example), followed by a period. This represents the revision to the current release number. Finally, the third number (the 1 in our example) is the bug fix to the revision.

Therefore, this is (going backwards) the first bug fix to the original of the second release version of the file.

Release stages

The vers editor can tell you (or set) the release information about a product. Release stages are the phases that a product goes through in its trip from a programmer's mind to a store shelf. Below, the different release stages are explained in more detail.

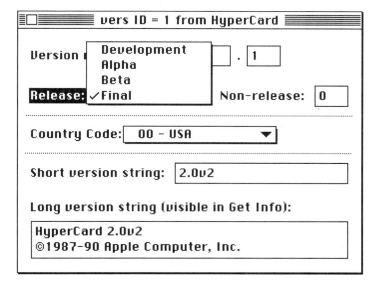

Figure 3 -

The vers editor, showing the Release pup-up menu.

- **Development:** Refers to the very first version of the software created. This is the stage where the programmers are thinking of the initial concepts, features, capabilities. This is also where the interface is usually created.

- **Alpha:** The product features having been defined in the development version, are now being tested to make sure that everything works Macintosh style.

- **ßeta:** This is where the product is supposed to be stable, and is undergoing final testing to eliminate as many bugs as possible — while still holding to the deadlines set by the Marketing Division of the company produc-

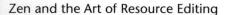

```
✓ 00 - USA
  01 - France
  02 - Britain
  03 - Germany
  04 - Italy
  05 - Netherlands
  06 - Belgium Lux.
  07 - Sweden
  08 - Spain
  09 - Denmark
  10 - Portugal
  11 - Fr. Canada
  12 - Norway
  13 - Israel
  14 - Japan
  15 - Australia
  16 - Arabia
  17 - Finland
  18 - Fr. Swiss
  19 - Gr. Swiss
  20 - Greece
  21 - Iceland
  22 - Malta
  23 - Cyprus
  24 - Turkey
  25 - Yugoslavia
  33 - India
  34 - Pakistan
  36 - It. Swiss
  40 - Anc. Greek
  41 - Lithuania
  42 - Poland
  43 - Hungary
  44 - Estonia
  45 - Latvia
  46 - Lapland
  47 - Faeroe Isl.
  48 - Iran
  49 - Russia
  50 - Ireland
  51 - Korea
  52 - China
  53 - Taiwan
  54 - Thailand
```

Figure 4 –

All the country codes available in *ResEdit*.

ing the software. This may be followed by a number, which indicates which beta release it is. Companies often do more than one. Note, however, the key phrase "supposed to be"

Finally...

- **Final:** Otherwise known as the Release version. This version is supposed to be complete in every respect. Not only will it do everything it's supposed to, but it will fail just as reliably when asked to do something the developers didn't anticipate you doing.

A non-release stage number is used when a programmer generates more than one version at any of the four release stages. For instance, there might be five beta releases before the product is actually released, and they would be numberd beta 1, beta 2, etc. The non-release stage number provides this information.

Country code

This gives your Mac the information it needs to know which country's operating system you are using. It makes it simple for developers to specify the language to be used by an application.

Currently, this does absolutely nothing. In System 7.0, it lets you know what country the application was written in—but it won't help you with translating the menus into English from Kanji.

While System 6 uses only the Long Version String, System 7 uses the Short Version String for the version information in Finder windows (seen when viewing by anything other than icon or small icon).

What can you use this for?

At first, it might seem as if this resource is only good for programmers who are assigning version numbers to their programs. However, there are many good uses of this resource for the average person. For instance, you could modify the vers resource of an application to reflect any modifications you might have made to the application itself. For instance, your Finder could say (in the Long Version String) something like "Extra modifications made by…" in its Get Info… dialog. Another useful idea is to use the Long Version String as a permanent comment box which isn't erased when rebuilding the Desktop. Simply type what you want into this area of the editor and save your changes.

vers overview

To access the vers resource:

- Open *ResEdit* and use it to open the program you wish to edit.
- Open the vers resource

To set the version number:

- Open vers ID# 1
- Enter the release number in the first field in the top row
- Enter the revision number in the second field in the top row
- Enter the bug fix number in the third field in the top row.

Brian Novack is one of the leaders of the Developers Forum on America Online. When he's not attending to his responsibilities online, he has been a contractor at Apple Computer and is now a student in St. Louis, Missouri. Among his programming accomplishments is Volume Manager, a shareware FKEY which allows you to adjust the speaker volume without waiting for the Control Panel to come up. He can be reached at AFA Brian on America Online.

Chapter Fifteen

Running With System 7

Moving
Deep in the mist
System 7

Running with System 7

With System 7 out, you will inevitably want to poke around at the resources in the System and Finder with ResEdit. Unfortunately, most of the new resources under System 7 do not have nice editors in ResEdit 2.1. As a result, you get a lot of very important resources opening as Hex editors. Nonetheless, there are some cool things you can do with them.

When is a menu not a menu?

When it's an fmnu, of course! Apple has taken out the MENU resource in the Finder and replaced it with a new type of resource, the fmnu (short for Finder MeNU). As with most of the new resources under System 7, it opens as a Hex editor (since *ResEdit* does not yet have editors for these resources) and looks very intimidating.

fmnu ID = 1252 from Finder cop!

```
000000    0001 0013 0000 04E4    □□□□□□□□
000008    0000 0000 0446 696C    □□□□□Fil
000010    6500 6E65 7720 C006    e□new ¿□
000018    4E00 0A4E 6577 2046    N□□New F
000020    6F6C 6465 7200 736F    older□so
000028    7065 1006 4F00 044F    pe□□□□□□
000030    7065 6E00 7370 7269    pen□spri
000038    1002 5000 0550 7269    □□P□□Pri
000040    6E74 636C 6F73 C006    ntclos¿□
000048    5700 0C43 6C6F 7365    W□□Close
000050    2057 696E 646F 7700    Window□
000058    7878 7830 0000 0000    xxx0□□□□
000060    012D 7369 6E66 1002    □-sinf□□
000068    4900 0847 6574 2049    I□□Get I
```

Figure 1 –

An fmnu resource, open to the File Menu.

Although it is difficult to add icons to these menu items, you can change the text of the item or add a command key. Let's take a closer look at Figure 1, fmnu resource #1252 from a copy of Finder 7.0. For instance, look at the fourth and fifth row of the editor, which shows the text "New Folder." If you look three spaces before this text, you will see the letter N. This is the command-key equivalent for this menu item.

To add your own command key, find the menu item you wish to edit and place the desired command key three spaces before the text of the menu item. Select the character which is already there in the right-hand column, and type in the new character. *ResEdit* will automatically create the hexadecimal equivalent for you.

For more information on working with menus in ResEdit, see Chapter 7, "Menus and You."

As you may have noticed, the fmnus are numbered differently from the MENU resources under System 6. Briefly, 1251 is the Apple menu, 1252 is the File menu, 1253 is the Edit menu, 1254 is the View menu, and 1255 is the Special menu.

Adding Quit to the Finder

If you've been using System 7 on a machine with two megabytes of RAM, you may have realized that memory quickly becomes an important issue. For System 6 users, this is not as much of a problem, since one can always start up under just the Finder, without MultiFinder running, but this is not an option under System 7. With *ResEdit*, however, one can easily add an option for quitting the Finder, directly from itself.

To get started, open up a copy of the Finder (which by this stage in this book you probably have a zillion of), and open up the fmnu resources. You should see a whole list. Since most Mac applications put "Quit" under the File menu, that's where we'll put ours. That's fmnu #1252, so go ahead and open that one. You should see something like Figure 1.

If you look along the right side of this window, you'll probably see some words you recognize, like "New Folder" or "Open." However, you'll also see some words you won't recognize, like "new " and "sope." First things first—you need a little bit of background about this menu.

One of the most advertised features of System 7 is AppleEvents. In most cases, this is not the kind of thing the end user cares about, except to know if an application supports them. Well, what are they? AppleEvents are messages and commands passed between applications. Applications which support AppleEvents can send a message, for instance, that would tell a program like Disinfectant to check some file for viruses. Similarly, you could send a complex message telling a program like Stuffit Deluxe 3.0 to compress a list of files, rename one of them, and then delete the originals. Though AppleEvents themselves aren't what people are excited about when they get System 7, the concept of Publish and Subscribe is, and this system is entirely controlled by AppleEvents. As a matter of fact, much of the System is run by AppleEvents, including what takes place whenever you choose a menu item.

Now let's get back to our fmnu and figure out how it relates. If you look at the menu again, you'll again notice words like "New Folder" and "Open." These are obviously the text of the menu items as you see them. Next to them, however, you'll see words like "new " and "sope." These are the AppleEvent codes for those menu items (not surprisingly, AppleEvent codes are four-letter words). For those of you who know a little about how AppleEvents are set up, these are actually the Event IDs for those AppleEvents, and the Event Class is "FNDR." (If you don't know what that meant, don't worry, it's not important to this discussion.)

To add a "Quit" menu item to our File menu, we need to send the Finder a "quit" AppleEvent. Fortunately, the Finder understands that particular AppleEvent. So, scroll to the end of the window, and you should see that it ends with the letter "m." This is actually the Print Window... menu item, but Apple uses a placeholder since that menu item can also say Print Desktop..., and they don't want to have the System rewriting resources constantly, since that would take time.

To insert our menu item, click at the end of the hex column (the middle one), and type the following string "7175 6974 8100 0000 0451 7569 7400" (don't type the spaces, they appear by themselves). In the right column, you'll notice that the words "quit" and "Quit" have appeared. Now you have a new menu item. But before you close the window, there's one more thing that you need to do. At the very top of the resource, there's a number showing how many items are in that menu. You need to change that to reflect your addition. So, go back to the top of the resource, and in the middle column, you'll notice that the second section in the top row says "0011." Select the 11 and replace it with the number 12. Now, install your new Finder, restart, and you'll have a Quit menu item.

Now, since this is a hack, there are some limitations as to how it works. For one thing, if you quit the Finder, and nothing else is running, the Finder will simply restart. That means that in order to use this effectively, you need to launch another application, switch back to the Finder, and then choose Quit. The other big problem is when you open one or two programs and have quit the Finder. If you want to get back to the Finder, you have to quit all the open applications. This can be tiresome. You'll also notice that your Apple menu is mostly gone. This is because the Apple menu is a folder in the Finder, and since you quit it, the System doesn't have anywhere to look for that folder. My suggestion is that you open any DAs you want first, and then quit the Finder. That way, you'll still have those desk accessories open.

So if it causes many problems, why would you want to do it? Well, for one thing, it releases about 350K of memory. If your program isn't happy in a cramped memory environment, this could give it the elbow room it needs. Another good reason to use the Quit command is to rebuild the Desktop. Everyone says that you rebuild your Desktop when you start up, right? Well, not quite. You are actually rebuild-

Figure 2 –

My File menu, with the Quit menu command

ing the Desktop when the Finder starts up. Therefore, if you quit the Finder and let it restart (which it does when no other applications are open), you can rebuild the Desktop just like you normally would. This saves time if you have a lot of extensions running at Startup.

There are a couple of things you may wish to do with this. Earlier in this section, there is information about adding command keys to Finder menus. Using this information, you could add a "Q" to be the command-key equivalent for this menu item. You may also want to add a separator line, so that your Quit is set off from everything else. To do this, look earlier in the same fmnu resource for a string which begins with "xxx0" and ends with "-" (this is in the rightmost column). Select this entire string, copy it, and then place the text right before the word "quit" in your new menu. Since you're adding a new item, you'll have to increase the item count to 0013 instead of 0012. Figure 3 shows you the fmnu resource with a separator line selected, ready to be copied. Figure 2, on the previous page, shows you the way I set up my File menu, so that you can get an idea of how the new menu item looks with a separator line.

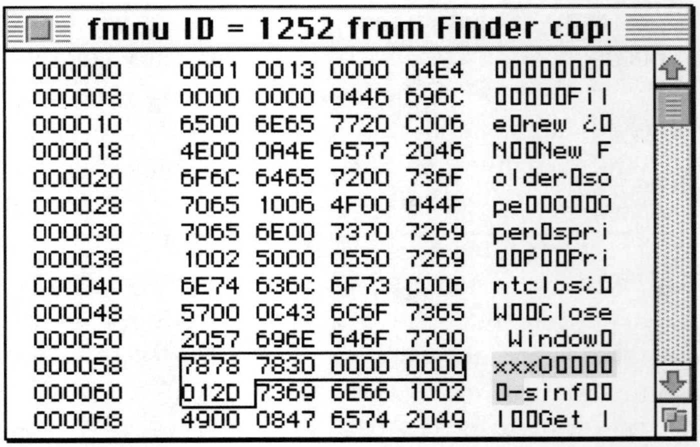

Figure 3 –

A separator line selected in fmnu #1252

```
 fmnu ID = 1252 from Finder cop!
000000   0001 0013 0000 04E4   00000000
000008   0000 0000 0446 696C   00000Fil
000010   6500 6E65 7720 C006   e0new ¿0
000018   4E00 0A4E 6577 2046   N00New F
000020   6F6C 6465 7200 736F   older0so
000028   7065 1006 4F00 044F   pe000000
000030   7065 6E00 7370 7269   pen0spri
000038   1002 5000 0550 7269   00P00Pri
000040   6E74 636C 6F73 C006   ntclos¿0
000048   5700 0C43 6C6F 7365   W00Close
000050   2057 696E 646F 7700   Window0
000058   7878 7830 0000 0000   xxx00000
000060   012D 7369 6E66 1002   0-sinf00
000068   4900 0847 6574 2049   I00Get I
```

Is your application "busy or missing"?

Under System 7, you may have noticed that when you double-click on a text file of some kind (and if you have *TeachText* on your hard drive), the System presents the dialog in Figure 4.

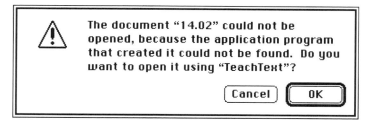

> ⚠️ The document "14.02" could not be opened, because the application program that created it could not be found. Do you want to open it using "TeachText"?
>
> [Cancel]   [OK]

Figure 4 –
Open with *TeachText*?

Thus, any text or PICT file can be opened and at least viewed with *TeachText*. This is similar functionality to the program known as *HandOff*, which allows you to set all *Microsoft Word* documents to open with *MacWrite II*, or something similar. Now, this capability is built into the system software, hidden in the fmap resource in the Finder.

To modify this, open up fmap ID# 17010 in a copy of the Finder.

```
 ▤□▤  fmap ID = 17010 from Finder copy ▤▤▤
 000000    5445 5854 7474 7874    TEXTttxt    ⇧
 000008    5049 4354 7474 7874    PICTttxt
 000010    0000 0000 0000 0000    □□□□□□□□
 000018
 000020
 000028                                        ⇩
 000030                                        ▥
```

Figure 5 –
fmap #17010 from Finder 7.0.

The first line contains eight characters, "TEXTttxt," and the second line contains a similar set of characters. The first four characters are the file type, which is text, and the last four characters are the signature (or creator) of the file you wish to open them. ttxt is the signature of *TeachText*. Translated, the first line of this resource says "Open any TEXT files with an application which has the signature ttxt."

Let's take a more practical example. *MacWrite* II has the capability to open a wide variety of files, and has many features for editing. One of these file types is *Microsoft Word 4.0*. So let's set up a line in our fmap which will provide the option of opening *Word* documents with *MacWrite II* when *Word* is not available.

First, we have to do some research. We need to know the file type of *Microsoft Word* documents. Fortunately, the tool we need is already in our hands—*ResEdit* itself. To get the file type, choose Get File/Folder Info... from the File menu, and find a *Word* document. (Don't worry if you can't. Just read along.) Hit the "Get Info" button after selecting the file. You will then see a dialog box similar to the one in Figure 6, below.

```
┌──────────────────────────────────────────────────┐
│ ☐▭▭▭▭▭  Info for Generic Word Document  ▭▭▭ │
├──────────────────────────────────────────────────┤
│  File │ Generic Word Document                    │
│  Type │ WDBN │         Creator │ MSWD │           │
│  ☐ System    ☐ Invisible   Color: │ Color 8 ▼│   │
│  ☐ On Desk   ☒ Inited      ☐ Bundle    ☐ Letter  │
│  ☐ Shared    ☐ No Inits    ☐ Alias     ☐ Stationery│
│  ☐ Always switch launch    ☐ Use custom icon     │
│ ─────────────────────────────────────────────────│
│  ☐ Resource map is read only        ☐ File Protect│
│  ☐ Printer driver is MultiFinder compatible ☐ File Busy│
│  Created │ 4/2/91  9:00:48 PM │      ☐ File Locked │
│  Modified │ 4/2/91  9:00:48 PM │                  │
│    Size   0 bytes in resource fork               │
│           2048 bytes in data fork                │
└──────────────────────────────────────────────────┘
```

Figure 6 –

The File Info... dialog for a *Word* document.

In the upper left, you'll see a field labeled "Type." That's the one we want. Jot down the four letter sequence, WDBN.

Next, we need to figure out the creator type for *MacWrite II*. Use Get File/Folder Info... again and get info on the application, *MacWrite II*. Write down the four-character sequence in the "Creator" field, MWII, which appears to the right of the Type field.

172

Okay, now that we've figured out these two things, go back to the fmap resource (#17010) in your copy of the Finder. Click right before the single row of 0s. Now type "WDBNMWII." It is very important for this to be by itself on the row, and for the last row to be nothing but 0s.

Beyond this, it is up to you how you wish to remap all of your applications. You should consult with your manuals to see how many different file types an application can open.

Aliases

One of the coolest features of System 7 is the ability to create aliases of files, folders, and even servers. The engineers at Apple were even smart enough to make a mechanism that would allow aliases to track their targets, most of the time.

Though there's not much to see, aliases can be opened with *ResEdit*. You can either drag one to the *ResEdit* icon (or an alias!) or choose Open... from the File menu in *ResEdit*. However, since double-clicking on an alias actually opens the target of the alias, you have to check the "Use Alias Instead of Original" box.

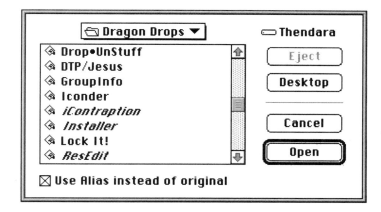

Figure 7 –

Opening an alias requires that you check the box at the bottom of ResEdit's Open... dialog box.

Once you've opened up the file, you'll notice that the only weird thing in an alias (unless you've pasted a custom icon on top) is an alis resource. Opening this will lead you to the hex editor. If you look through the right column, you can see that the alias actually contains the pathname of the file that it points to, which makes sense.

```
alis ID = 0 from ResEdit
000070    0000 0000 00B4 A43B    00000¥§;
000078    07A1 4150 504C 5253    0°APPLRS
000080    4544 0003 0002 0000    ED000000
000088    0011 0000 0000 0000    00000000
000090    0000 0000 0000 0000    00000000
000098    0007 5265 7345 6469    00ResEdi
0000A0    7400 0001 0004 0000    t0000000
0000A8    0092 0002 0018 5468    0í0000Th
0000B0    656E 6461 7261 3A52    endara:R
0000B8    6573 4564 6974 3A52    esEdit:R
0000C0    6573 4564 6974 0009    esEdit00
0000C8    00A8 00A8 6166 706D    0®0®afpm
0000D0    0000 0000 0003 0018    00000000
0000D8    0039 0059 0075 0095    090YOu0ï
```

Figure 8 –
The alis resource

What can you use this for? Well, one way to befuddle aliases is to change the hard drive name on a Macintosh. If you're an alias fanatic, you probably have lots of aliases, and you don't want to go through and make aliases of everything all over again. With *ResEdit*, you can just go through each of your aliases (yes, you do still have to do this), and change the alis resource so that it contains the name of the new hard drive. To do this, just find the name of your old hard drive in the right column, select it, and replace it with the new name of your hard drive. You'll notice that there are usually several copies of your hard drive's name. That's because the alias doesn't just contain the pathname, it also holds the name of your server and zone and all the other elements of your network address. It will also contain the name you set up in the Sharing Setup control panel, so that the alias knows who the owner is. Change all of these if you need to support network access.

Where to find those custom icons.

One of the purely cosmetic features of System 7 is the ability to create custom icons for individual folders through the Get Info... box in the Finder. Many people now know that they can simply select that icon in the dialog and, if they have a picture in the Clipboard, paste a new image on top. Many people have wondered where this is stored. The main reason people want to know is that System 7 makes really bad masks for certain colors (some yellows, reds, and greens, mostly). In addition, some people find that the small versions of the icons come out looking pretty bad, so they want to play with that specific resource to make it more aesthetically pleasing.

The icon information for a folder (and a hard drive) is stored in an invisible file within the folder itself, whose name is simply "Icon." Though you can't see it from the Finder, *ResEdit* will show it, and you can open it and play with it if you need to. The file will have an entire icon family of resources, even if you have a black & white monitor. Thus, you can make whatever changes need to be made. In the event that your colors got messed up, you'll want to fill in the Mask, which you'll notice is poorly made. If you want to edit a small icon, open up the ics8, ics4, or ics# resource, as appropriate.

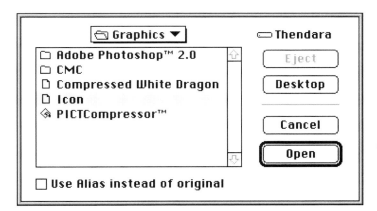

Figure 9 –

A Standard File dialog box, showing an invisible Icon file within a folder.

If you've pasted a custom icon onto a file or application, the System makes an icon family in that file whose resource number is -16455. If you need to change some aspect, open up whichever resource you need to with that ID number.

By the way, many people are confused that they can't simply copy an icl8 or whatever onto the Clipboard and then paste it onto a picture. The reason for this is that the Clipboard can only hold pictures, text, and sound. *ResEdit* maintains its own special Clipboard for moving resources around. Thus, to copy an icon onto the Clipboard, you have to go all the way into the icon editor, select the actual image, and copy that. Since that is a graphic, it will work.

For more information about editing icons in general, read the sections dealing with regular icons and color icons earlier in this book.

Disabling the ZoomRects

As you may have read in the section dealing with the LAYO resource at the beginning of this book, System 6 users have the capacity to disable the animated zoom rectangles which appear every time a window is opened or closed. With the new Finder under System 7, this is no longer easy to get to. Nonetheless, some people have figured out where that information is. To disable your ZoomRects (as they are fondly called), open up a copy of the Finder, and go to CODE resource number 4. *ResEdit* will tell you it is compressed, but you need to decompress it to make this change (everything has a price, after all). When you open it up, you'll be faced with *ResEdit*'s famous hex editor. If you don't know how to use this, you may want to take a second to read Appendix 2, "Using the Hex Editor."

Once you're all set up, choose Find Offset... from the Find menu. Type into the dialog box that you want to find

0078. When *ResEdit* gets you there, select the following characters (in the hex column): 48E7 1F38. Change these characters to 6000 00E6, by typing over the old characters.

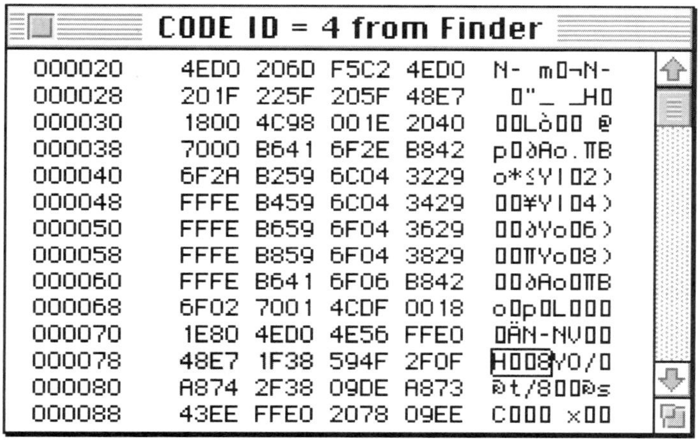

```
▓▓ ▓▓▓▓▓▓     CODE ID = 4 from Finder ▓▓▓▓▓▓
000020     4ED0 206D F5C2 4ED0    N- m0¬N-        ⬆
000028     201F 225F 205F 48E7    0"_ _H0
000030     1800 4C98 001E 2040    00Lò00 @
000038     7000 B641 6F2E B842    p00Ao.πB
000040     6F2A B259 6C04 3229    o*‹Y|02)
000048     FFFE B459 6C04 3429    00¥Y|04)
000050     FFFE B659 6F04 3629    00ðYo06)
000058     FFFE B859 6F04 3829    00πYo08)
000060     FFFE B641 6F06 B842    00ðAo0πB
000068     6F02 7001 4CDF 0018    o0p0L000
000070     1E80 4ED0 4E56 FFE0    0ÄN-NV00
000078     48E7 1F38 594F 2F0F    H008Yo/0        ⬇
000080     A874 2F38 09DE A873    Ðt/800Ðs
000088     43EE FFE0 2078 09EE    C000 ×00        ▨
```

Figure 10 –

The CODE resource, with the important characters selected, ready to be changed.

Install your new Finder, restart, and you will be rid of the annoying ZoomRects!

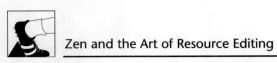

Chapter Sixteen

QuickTips: Cool Things to Know

Listen,
all creeping things
the bell of QuickTips

Tip #1: The *ResEdit* "RMAP" resource

Have you ever had the situation where, upon examining a strange resource in the *ResEdit* hex editor, you were certain the resource was really a common one, just that it bore an unusual resource type? *ResEdit* actually has a mechanism where you can map resource types from one kind to another. This is sometimes called aliasing.

What aliasing allows you to do is specify that resouce type A is to be treated the same as resource type B. Whenever you open a type A resource, *ResEdit* will use type B's picker and editors.

For example, let's look at an unusual resource of type "N&CS" as normally seen in *ResEdit*.

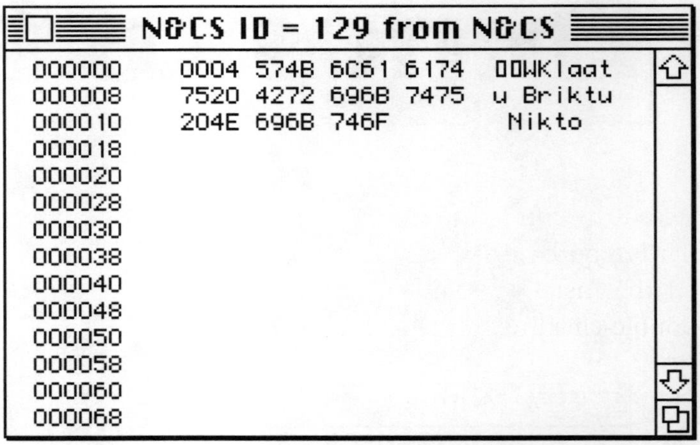

```
N&CS ID = 129 from N&CS
000000    0004 574B 6C61 6174    □□WKlaat
000008    7520 4272 696B 7475    u Briktu
000010    204E 696B 746F            Nikto
000018
000020
000028
000030
000038
000040
000048
000050
000058
000060
000068
```

Figure 1 –

The resource of type N&CS as seen through the eyes of *ResEdit*.

Since *ResEdit* has no special templates or editors for this resource, it just uses the Standard Hex editor to display it. However, closer examination reveals that this resource looks remarkably like an "STR " resource. (The space after STR is part of its name.) Wouldn't it be nice if we could view it as an "STR " resource? Well, we can; however, it means modifying *ResEdit* itself.

If you open a copy of *ResEdit 2.1* itself, using *ResEdit 2.1*, you'll discover a resource type called "RMAP." (See figure below) This is *ResEdit*'s Resource MAPping (or aliasing) mechanism.

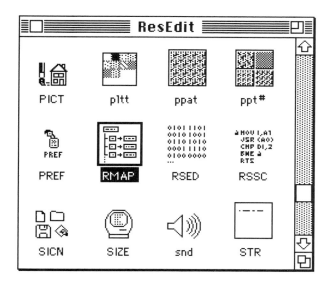

Figure 2 –

ResEdit, opened by *ResEdit*.

There are already RMAP resources installed in *ResEdit* for all the common resources that are identical to standard resource types, but bear different types. You can see all the installed RMAP resources in *ResEdit* merely by double-clicking on the RMAP icon.

ID	Size	Name
200	40	"PREC"
201	8	"FCMT"
202	8	"MACS"
203	8	"minf"
204	24	"INTL"
205	8	"cmnu"
206	8	"mctb"
207	8	"ics#"

Figure 3 –

Some of the RMAPs in *ResEdit*.

To add your own custom RMAP, merely choose Duplicate, or create a new RMAP resource. Then double-click that new resource to open the RMAP editor. Figure 4 is an example of the RMAP resource just created for the "N&CS" resource we suspected was actually an "STR " resource.

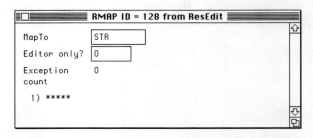

Figure 4 –

The RMAP "editor," with the relevant info already typed in for making an N&CS open as an STR.

Notice that the "Map To" field has the "STR " resource type entered. This is the resource type we wish to use to look at the N&CS resource. (Note the all-important trailing space character; all types must have four characters!) The "Editor only?" field has been left at zero, and the "Exception" list has zero entries. Generally, it's best to leave these last two items alone.

Finally, it's important that your new RMAP resource be named properly. *ResEdit* uses the name of the RMAP resource to determine what resources to watch for when performing mapping. Therefore, the name of our "N&CS" map resource must be "N&CS." The name of the resource is changed in the Get Resource Info... dialog.

Figure 5 –

The Get Resource Info... dialog box for the RMAP we just created.

Now that we have created, modified, and named our "N&CS" map resource in a copy of *ResEdit 2.1*, we save our changes, and then quit *ResEdit*. Upon launching our modified copy of *ResEdit 2.1*, we can now view the odd "N&CS" resource. *ResEdit* will use our new map resource to allow us to view it as a regular "STR " resource. Figure 6 shows what the final result looks like.

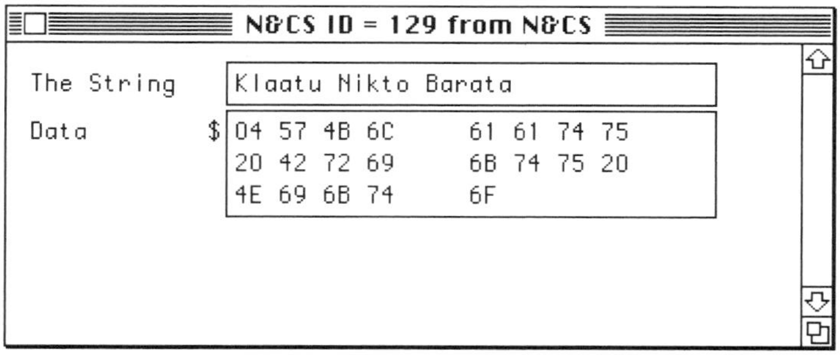

```
≣□≣▭≣≣▬▬≣ N&CS ID = 129 from N&CS ≣▬▬≣        ⇧
  The String     Klaatu Nikto Barata
  Data        $ 04 57 4B 6C    61 61 74 75
                20 42 72 69    6B 74 75 20
                4E 69 6B 74    6F
                                                ⇩
                                                ⌻
```

Figure 6 –

The N&CS resource, opened as a STR resource.

We can now view the "N&CS" resource in a much friendlier fashion all of the time, and it can be safely edited as well. *ResEdit*'s built-in "STR " editor will take care of all the details, such as the hidden length byte of the string.

Tip #2: Giving resources icons in *ResEdit* itself

By now, you're accustomed to seeing the icons *ResEdit* uses to represent the various icons. ICONs, MENUs, DLOGs, and even the hex editor have their own icons inside *ResEdit*. But what if you've got a resource that doesn't have an icon? This means that it doesn't have an editor, and you'll be shown the hex icon instead.

If you've created your own templates or copied one from a friend, or you've set up an RMAP resource (see Tip #1), you may want to give it an icon so that you'll remember what it is.

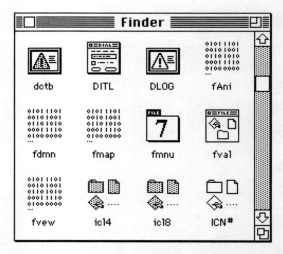

Figure 1 –

The Finder with an icon for the fmnu resource.

To add an icon to a resource, double-click on the ICON icon in *ResEdit* itself. Choose **Create New Resource** from the **Resource** menu. Edit the icon so it looks the way you want it to. Now, close the editor and click once on your new icon. Choose **Get Resource Info...** from the **Resource** menu, and change the name of the icon so that it matches the name of the resource. Save your changes, and it's all done. Any time *ResEdit* sees a resource with that type, it will display your icon for it. I used this technique to create an icon for the fmnu resource.

Tip #3: Adding your own colors to *ResEdit*

As you've been editing ppats and color icons, you have probably seen the Color menu, which allows you to change the colors on *ResEdit*'s color palette. Usually, this only has a few options in it. "Apple Icon Colors" is a set of colors which represents Apple's 34 recommended colors for making icons. "Standard 256 Colors" is the set of colors which shows all the colors the System normally uses. You can switch between them using this menu.

However, there may be times when you want to add your own colors to this menu. For instance, if you like blues, you may want to make a color palette with a lot of blues on it. To do this, you need to use a resource known as the clut.

Open up a copy of your *ResEdit* preferences (in the System Folder under System 6 and in the Preferences Folder inside the System Folder under System 7), and create a clut resource using **Create New Resource...** in the **Resource** menu. Since there are no cluts installed, *ResEdit* will ask you what kind of resource to make. Type in "clut," and *ResEdit* will bring up a new clut in its editor, as seen below.

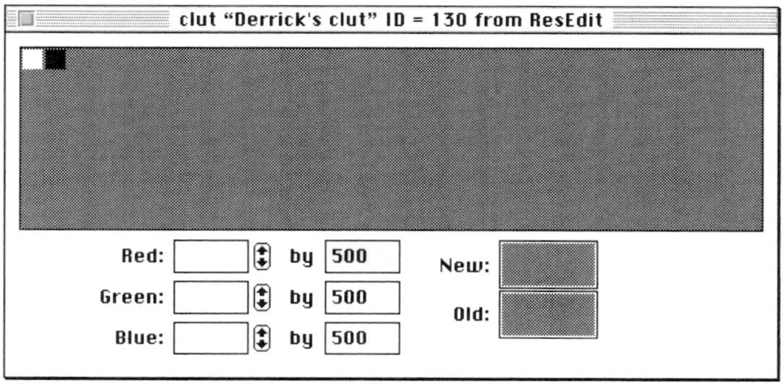

Figure 1 –
The clut editor

There will only be two colors in your new clut: black and white. To add a new color, choose **Insert New Color** from the **Resource** menu. This will make a new black square. Black and white are pretty boring, so you probably want to change the color. To do so, you can double-click on a square, or you can click once and choose Open Color Picker... to choose which color you want. Be sure to give your new clut a name so that it shows up properly in the menu, and you're all done.

Once you've finished making your clut, go ahead and install your new Preferences file (you may want to keep a copy of the other one) by changing its name or deleting your old one and putting your new one in (make sure it's named "ResEdit Preferences" or *ResEdit* won't pay any attention to it. Now, when you go to edit any color resource (excluding icon families, due to a quirk in *ResEdit*), you will see that your Color menu has your new entry in it. Now you can get a palette that has just the right shade of green or whatever you desire.

This does not always have the best results, however. Since the System uses its own clut, your custom colors will get mapped to a similar color in the system palette. Since this makes adding your own custom colors pointless, you may want to consider editing the system clut. To do this, open a copy of the System and then open clut #9. Double-click on the color you wish to change, and use the color picker to choose your new color.

Figure 2 –
The color picker.

Once you've done this, you'll be able to use that color in all color resources (including icon families, since the "Standard 256 Colors" is drawn directly from the System), and it won't be mapped to a similar color. This is often the better route, but it causes you to lose the original colors until you re-install.

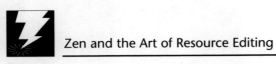

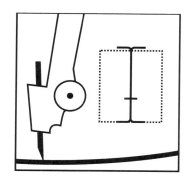

A Quick Review of the Paint Tools

*Beyond 24-bit
gray kites
in twilight.*

A quick review of the paint tools

Former versions of *ResEdit* have had very limited bitmap editors. The icon windows, for instance, had two choices of tools: the pencil and the selection rectangle, or marquee. The pencil was the pointer, and it would make a black pixel white and a white pixel black. The marquee was available when holding down the Shift key. With this, you could move parts of the icon or use the Clipboard for copying and pasting pieces of artwork.

ResEdit 2.1, however, features much more advanced editors. Now, all the bitmap resources have a wider variety of tools to choose from.

These tools will be very familiar to those who use paint programs frequently, but a quick review might be handy for those who don't use these applications as often.

The ability to cut, copy, and paste objects from one application to another is one of the Mac's greatest features. Recall, however, that something needs to be selected before it can be cut or copied. This is the function of both the lasso tool and the marquee. The marquee draws out a rectangular area to be cut or copied. Anything within (and directly under) the borders of this rectangle will be cut or copied. To use this tool, click and drag the mouse. This will draw out the rectangle. You can then choose Cut or Copy from the Edit menu. Sometimes, however, you'll find that the marquee is too limited. Perhaps you want to select an area, but a rectangle would select stuff you don't want. This is where the lasso comes in handy. Rather than drawing a rectangle, the lasso allows you to outline the area which will be selected. Again, click and drag, but this time draw the border of the area you want to select. (This may be a bit difficult for people like myself, whose freehand abilities are sorely lacking, but a little practice will make it much easier.) Now this area is ready to cut or copy to the Clipboard. As a useful shortcut, double-clicking on the selection rectangle in the tool area will select the whole editing panel.

The next tool is the pencil tool. This is used to turn "off" or "on" individual pixels (a pixel is "on" if it is black, and "off" if it is white). The bitmap editors of *ResEdit* show you much enlarged pixels for easy editing, and the pencil tool turns these large squares off and on. Click on a white pixel to make it black, and vice versa (the pencil tool is slightly different with color editors, but that is covered in the color icon sections). In older versions of *ResEdit*, this was the only tool or editing the icons. Thankfully, this is no longer the case!

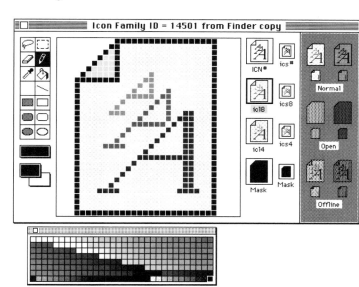

Figure 1 –

The paint tools in *ResEdit*'s icl8 editor .

One of the new tools is the paint bucket. In all of the editors, you'll see a pattern palette (usually a pop-up menu) and a color palette. You can select these patterns simply by clicking on them. With the paint bucket, you can fill an entire area with the pattern which you have selected. The "hot spot" (active part) of the cursor is the very tip of the spilling paint. Therefore, to fill a small area, make sure the hot spot is in this area. If you accidentally fill an area (a common enough mistake), you can fix this by immediately choosing Undo from the Edit menu. If you've clicked somewhere else after making this mistake, however, you cannot undo.

This brings us to the next tool, the eraser. The eraser, as its name implies, will "erase" pixels. It does this by turning off any pixel underneath it when the mouse button is down. It will always make the pixels white, even in the color editors. Use it by clicking and dragging it around inside the editor. In tight corners, you should be careful about using this tool. For areas like this, you can use the pencil to turn off the pixels. *ResEdit's* eraser is slightly improved from the normal eraser. With most paint programs, you can't see what's under the eraser. In *ResEdit*, however, the eraser rectangle is transparent. Similarly to the selection rectangle, double-clicking on the eraser tool erases the whole editing area.

Another useful tool is the line tool. With this tool, you can make straight lines quickly and easily. However, this may not produce the effect you want. When the line tool makes "straight" lines, it actually approximates a line. If the line you wish to make is 45°, 90°, or 180°, it will be a straight line. However, any other angle will produce a line which looks jagged. Despite the way it looks, it is nonetheless the straightest line which can be drawn on the computer screen.

The final tools are the shape tools. There are six of these below the other tools: three shaded and three empty. Each of these tools draws the shape it looks like (rectangle, rectangle with rounded corners, and ovals). The shaded tools fill the shape with whatever pattern is selected. The hollow tools just draw the shape, and you will be able to see the pixels "underneath."

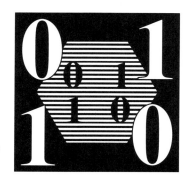

Appendix Two

Using the Hex Editor

The midnight beep,
rarely heard,
came sixteen times today.

Using the hex editor

ResEdit was designed to edit some of the more common resources in programs and the System. However, every program has its own resources, and *ResEdit* might not know how to deal with them. As a result, *ResEdit* has a last-resort editor known quite simply as the hex editor. All it does is show you the hexadecimal information within a resource.

Despite the fact that this editor looks pretty scary when you get into it, it's really not that bad. To see what it's like, open up any WDEF resource in a copy of your System file. These are the resources which describe the way a window looks, but that won't be evident. What you'll see is something like Figure 1, below.

```
╔════════ WDEF ID = 1 from System ════════╗
 000000    600A 0000 5744 4546   `□□□WDEF    ▲
 000008    0001 000A 4E56 FFE2   □□□□NV□□    ▒
 000010    48E7 1C18 0C6E 0002   H□□□□n□□    ▒
 000018    000C 6E00 00BA 0C6E   □□n□□∫□n    ▒
 000020    0000 000C 6B00 00B0   □□□□k□□∞    ▒
 000028    2055 2F10 0C78 3FFF    U/□□×?□    ▒
 000030    028E 53EE FFE2 6234   □éS□□□b4    ▒
 000038    6100 00B8 486E FFE4   a□□☐Hn□□    ▒
 000040    AA19 486E FFEA AA1A   ™□Hn□□™□    ▒
 000048    42A7 4267 2F2E 000E   BßBg/.□□    ▒
 000050    486F 0006 AA42 544F   Ho□□™BTO    ▒
 000058    205F 2050 2068 0008    _ P h□□    ▼
 000060    2D48 FFF0 A029 2D50   −H□□↑)−P    ◆
 000068    FFF4 6006 2F38 09DE   □□`□/8□□    ▣
╚══════════════════════════════════════════╝
```

Figure 1 –
The hex editor.

The rightmost column is the only one which might have legible information, though it still probably looks like gibberish. This is the ASCII column, which shows you (in between garbage characters) the English equivalents of the hexadecimal code. *ResEdit* sometimes does a really nice job of this, but other times it looks like nonsense. The middle column is the hexadecimal column. It does not contain any information which would be useful to the average user (since most average users don't think in hexadecimal). The middle four columns shows the offset, in bytes, from the beginning of the resource.

Real uses of the hex editor

Usually, you will not need to deal with the hex editor, but in the event that you need to (for instance, if you want to do some of the System 7 stuff we will talk about later), there are a couple things to know. When you're in the hex editor, you get a Find menu. This menu allows you to find by hexadecimal, ASCII, or offset within the resource. That way, you can quickly go to the appropriate area.

You can also, obviously, edit the text within this resource. However, there are a few little quirks about this. For one thing, when you're typing in either the hexadecimal or ASCII column (you can't type into the offset column), *ResEdit* will translate what you type into the other column. For instance, if you're typing in the ASCII area, the hex column will also fill to represent the characters you're typing. However, you can only actually type into one area at a time. If you want to copy and paste information somewhere else in a resource, you can only paste hex into the hex column and ASCII into the ASCII column (actually, you can paste hex into the ASCII column, but it's no longer hex when you do so; *ResEdit* converts it into ASCII).

Typing in text has some other differences from what you're used to in a word processor. For one, you cannot put a return into either the hex or ASCII columns. When you type return in either column, you are moved to the equivalent location in the other column. Another change is seen when you're typing into the hex column. Since each ASCII character is represented by two hex characters, when you type in something like "5" into the hex editor, *ResEdit* puts down "05." If you type "5D," it will first put down "05" and then move the 5 over and tack on the D, giving "5D." While this may be more distracting, you should keep it in mind if you use the Delete key. The Delete key does not remove one character at a time in the hex column; it removes two characters in one fell swoop. As a result, don't hit the Delete key twice to get rid of "5D."

Beyond that, there's not much more you can do with the hex editor. If you ever wish to open a resource in the hex editor, but it has an editor within *ResEdit* (which opens up first), hold down the Option key.

Installing Editors

Dozing on keyboard,
smoke from power supply
drifts through the fan.

Adding editors to *ResEdit*

One of *ResEdit*'s nicest features is the ability to install new editors into *ResEdit* itself. With this capability, you can increase *ResEdit*'s functionality by giving yourself the ability to edit resources you might not otherwise be able to edit, or to more easily edit some resource.

Editors are available from online services and user groups such as BMUG. Some of the most popular ones out there now allow you to edit snd resources, acurs, aliases, System 7 keyboard icons, CODE resources (remember that *ResEdit* is a programmer's tool), and even the Balloon Help for icons in the Finder. Two of these, snds and acurs, are included on the disk which came with the book.

To install these editors, you must open a copy of your ResEdit Preferences file. This file will either be in your System Folder (under System 6) or in your Preferences folder (located in your System Folder under System 7). Once this file is opened, open the file which contains the editor you wish to install. Figure 1 shows the file containing the acur editor from the disk which came with this book.

Figure 1 –

The acur editor from the disk included with this book.

198

Now choose Select All from the Edit menu. All the resources will highlight. Copy these resources, and then paste them into the ResEdit Preferences file. Now replace your old ResEdit Preferences with your new one, and restart *ResEdit*. Now, when you open any acur resource, you'll be using this editor.

There are three editors included on this disk. The acur editor allows you to easily edit animated cursors. The snd editor allows a graphic representation of the snd resources, which *ResEdit* has always shown as hexadecimal before. The fmap template allows you to easily edit fmap resource #17010, which controls System 7's file substitution. For more information about each of these editors, read the files which come with them. For information on using the fmap resource, read "Getting a Running Start with System 7."

In actuality, you could place the editors directly into *ResEdit*. However, it is a better idea to put them in the Preferences file. If you kept your editors inside *ResEdit* itself, you would lose them as soon as you got a newer version of *ResEdit*. However, you should keep a backup copy of your Preferences file around, in case it gets damaged (which it sometimes does).

If you want to find some more editors, prowl around online services such as America Online. Do searches for words like "ResEdit," "Editor," and "Template." These will usually unearth some good selections.

Types and Creators

by Chris Holmes

Buddha's Nirvana,
beyond type,
and creator.

Types and Creators

The deceptively simple power provided by the Type and Creator resources drives what is easily one of the nicest, yet most subtle features of the Macintosh interface: The ability to open a document directly, rather than via the application that created it. This feature has been incorporated into nearly every graphical user interface ever since. The System is able to do this by using two four-letter codes for each file—a Type and a Creator.

Creator codes represent the application which that particular file belongs to. Every file associated with a program, including the program itself, has the same creator code. Types, on the other hand, are associated with a specific kind of file. For instance, *MacWrite*'s type is APPL, indicating that it is an application, which can be opened by double-clicking on the file. The type of a *MacWrite II* document is MW2D. MacWrite can also create files containing unformatted text, which have a type of TEXT.

When you double-click on a document, the Finder looks in an invisible file called the Desktop. The Desktop holds a list that links each file to its creator. The Finder looks at the creator code of that document and then finds the application with the same creator code. Then it opens the application and tells it to open your document, also telling the program the file's type. If you don't have an application to match that creator code, you'll get a dialog saying that the program is not available, like the one in Figure 1, below.

Figure 1 –

The System tells you that the creator application of a particular document is not available.

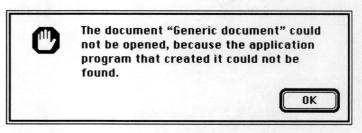

The document "Generic document" could not be opened, because the application program that created it could not be found.

OK

Occasionally, this gets messed up. The surest sign of this is that you no longer have icons, or have different icons, for a particular document. This tells you that the Desktop file has crossed its wires. To fix this, you can rebuild the Desktop file by holding down the Option and Command keys as you start your Macintosh. Keep in mind that rebuilding your desktop will erase all of the text in the Comments field of all Get Info windows on that volume.

Though the files a program creates have unique creator codes (which must be registered by Apple to prevent two programs from having the same creator code), the files it creates do not necessarily have unique types. In fact, several file types have become a standard for exchanging information between applications. For example, TEXT is unformatted text, PICT files are graphic images created by programs like *MacDraw* and *SuperPaint*, PIC2 files are PICT files with color information, TIFF files contain high-resolution, bit-mapped images, and MooV files contain QuickTime data.

To find out what the type and creator are for anything, use Get File/Folder Info… in *ResEdit*'s File menu. This brings up a standard file dialog box, which you can use to navigate to the file or application you wish to investigate. *ResEdit* will return a dialog box like that in Figure 2, below.

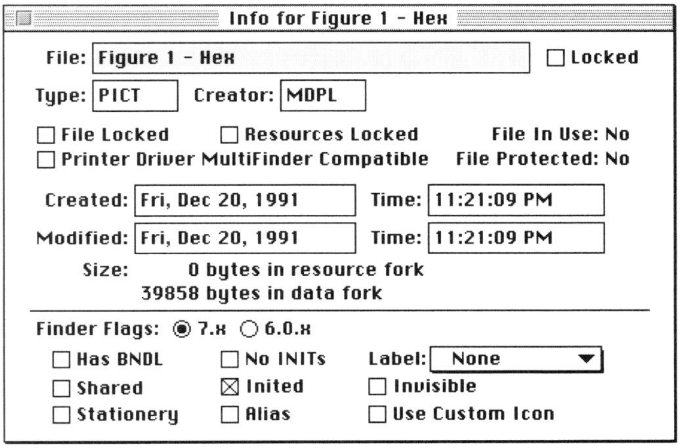

Info for Figure 1 - Hex	

File: Figure 1 - Hex   ☐ Locked

Type: PICT   Creator: MDPL

☐ File Locked   ☐ Resources Locked   File In Use: No
☐ Printer Driver MultiFinder Compatible   File Protected: No

Created: Fri, Dec 20, 1991   Time: 11:21:09 PM

Modified: Fri, Dec 20, 1991   Time: 11:21:09 PM

Size: 0 bytes in resource fork
39858 bytes in data fork

Finder Flags: ◉ 7.x ○ 6.0.x

☐ Has BNDL   ☐ No INITs   Label: None ▼
☐ Shared   ☒ Inited   ☐ Invisible
☐ Stationery   ☐ Alias   ☐ Use Custom Icon

Figure 2 –

Get File/Folder Info…
dialog box.

The check boxes are there for the System's use, and you will not need to change them.

So how can you use this dialog? For one thing, if you'd like to open any file in a certain application (for instance, if you have a TEXT file you'd like to open in *MacWrite II*, instead of getting Figure 1's dialog box whenever you try to open it), you can use the Get File/Folder Info… dialog to change its creator code to MWII. It's usually not a good idea to change the type for a file, since applications tend to do certain things with certain types of files. However, if you want something to always open in *ResEdit*, for example, you can make the creator for that file RSED and change its type to rsrc. After you're done, when you double-click on that file, *ResEdit* will open it as a regular *ResEdit* document. This can usually not be done for any file and any program; *ResEdit* is an exception. Most applications put some kind of private information into a file. Thus, while you can make all *Microsoft Word* documents launch *MacWrite II*, *MacWrite II* will not know how to deal with the information in the files. Although many applications have "translators" which will open certain kinds of documents, this has to be done from within the program itself.

However, in System 7, the Finder's "intelligence" was enhanced, allowing it to substitute another application for one it can't find. So if you create a TEXT document with *MacWrite* and then throw away the *MacWrite* application, the Finder will ask if you would like to open the document with another application that can open text documents, like *TeachText*, which is the default substitution for TEXT– and PICT–type documents. You can use *ResEdit* to specify which applications will be substituted for each type of document. (See Chapter 15, "Running With System 7" for more information about adding your own substitutions or editing the ones which already exist.)

Chris Holmes moved out of Central Pennsylvania and into California just over six-months ago to find his fame and fortune in the Land of the Rainbow Sunset and is now part of Dantz Development Corporation's Technical Support team.

Application Program	Creator
Acta	otln
Canvas 3	DAD2
Clarisworks	BOBO
Compact Pro	CPCT
Excel	XCEL
Filemaker Pro	FMPR
Freehand 3	FHA3
HyperCard	WILD
Illustrator 3	ART3
Illustrator 88	ARTZ
MacDraw	MDRW
MacDraw II	MDPL
MacDraw Pro	dPro
MacPaint	MPNT
MacWrite	MACA
MacWrite II	MWII
Microsoft Word	MSWD
Microsoft Works 2	PSI2
Pagemaker 4	ALD4
Photoshop	8BIM
Quark XPress	XPRS
ResEdit	RSED
SoundEdit	SFX!
StuffIt Deluxe	SIT!
SuperPaint	SPNT
TeachText	ttxt
WordPerfect	SSIW
WriteNow	nX^n

Figure 3 –

This table shows some of the most common programs, and their creators.

Appendix Five

About BMUG...

BMUG is an educational non-profit organization dedicated to collecting, evaluating, and disseminating information about graphical interface computers. We give users information to help them use their computers efficiently and painlessly. BMUG is not affiliated with any manufacturer, and represents the interests of thousands of users in the United States and in over 50 countries around the world. We offer local activities in the San Francisco Bay Area and services for members everywhere. All our meetings are free and open to the public; our disk library is available for sale to anyone. However, technical assistance, newsletters and our electronic information services are provided for members only.

Membership

BMUG is financed by membership dues and the sale of our educational products. In order to remain objective in our evaluations of the computer industry, we do not accept advertising in our publications. The majority of BMUG members renew year after year. Read on to find out what keeps them coming back.

Each one-year BMUG membership includes two issues of our highly acclaimed *BMUG Newsletter*, at least one account on the BMUG BBS, and free access to our technical Helpline.

All our meetings, as well as the software library, *Disk Catalog*, PD ROM, back issues of the *Newsletter*, and other BMUG publications are available to non-members.

Our goal is to provide you with the widest possible array of useful information. Find out why *MicroTimes* listed BMUG as one of the 100 most important influences in the computer industry and said, *"BMUG is what every user group dreams of becoming."* Please support us by joining BMUG.

BMUG membership packages

One-Year Individual – $40

- Two issues of the *Newsletter* per year
- One BBS account
- Unlimited access to the Helpline for one year

One-Year Company – $100

- Two copies of each *Newsletter* per year
- Eight BBS accounts
- Unlimited access to the Helpline for 25 people for one year

To contact BMUG

Announcement Line: ....510 / 849-9114
      recorded messages about BMUG activities

Business Line: ....510 / 549-2684
      mail-order and membership questions

FAX: ....510 / 849-9026
      if you'd rather send a note

Addresses

BMUG mailing address:

    1442A Walnut Street #62
    Berkeley, CA 94709–1496

BMUG office address:

    2055 Center Street
    in downtown Berkeley

Online

The BMUG multi-line electronic Bulletin Board System (BBS) is the crossroads of a larger international network, and an information resource in itself.

It is one of the premier nodes in the EchoMac network on FidoNet and is also part of UseNet and UUCP Mail on the InterNet. Each of these non-profit networks is monitored by tens of thousands of computer users in America and abroad.

Most of the latest publicly distributable software is available online, and is subjected to the same intense scrutiny for viruses as our disk-based software library. Our multi-line capability gives you fast access 20 hours a day (our BBS processes mail with other systems from 2:30–3:30 PM and 5:30–6:30 AM Pacific time), all lines support 300, 1200, or 2400 baud at 510/849-2684; 9600 baud access at 510 / 849-1795; Courier HST Access at 510/849-3844.

Publications

Newsletter

Twice a year, BMUG publishes a newsletter full of interesting articles on a variety of subjects. Unlike other user group newsletters — and unlike other Macintosh publications — the *BMUG Newsletter* is typically over 400 pages long and contains no advertising. Our newsletter is the heart of our activities; it serves as a medium for the exchange of information and contains some of the most honest, insightful commentary in the entire computer industry.

Joining BMUG is the only way to get the *BMUG Newsletter,* and we work hard to live up to our members' expectations.

BMUG Shareware Disk Catalog, Third Edition

A comprehensive guide to BMUG's general software library: descriptions, icons, and author information for thousands of programs and files.

This 650+ page book is the definitive reference for publicly distributable software. It's organized by disk and has handy indices which allow you to locate any application or file quickly. Call the business office for price and ordering information.

Meetings & SIGs

BMUG's Main Meeting is held every Thursday, and is attended by several hundred people. The main meetings are held on the UC Berkeley campus. We also offer various Special Interest Groups (SIGs), which focus on particular topics or issues. SIGs meet in the BMUG office unless otherwise specified. All our meetings are free and open to the public; beginners are always welcome.

Helpline

BMUG attempts to supply unlimited technical support for our members over the phone, through online informations services, and via FAX. BMUG is in constant contact with thousands of computer users who are doing virtually everything imaginable with their machines. We have an incredible knowledge base to draw upon in solving your problems. We have been doing Macintosh tech support as long as anyone. We can answer virtually any Macintosh question, simple or advanced—just call. We specialize in both beginners' questions and hard-to-find technical tips.

Software library

BMUG maintains one of the most comprehensive, up-to-date collections of publicly distributable software. Our library has hundreds of 800K disks. *Publicly distributable* means the author has given permission for the software to be copied and distributed freely. The majority of this software is *shareware*, which you should pay the author for if you keep and find it useful. Since shareware itself is typically quite inexpensive, BMUG tries to keep its disk prices low, so you will have money left over to pay for the software you use. Individual software prices are shown in shareware files and the *Shareware Disk Catalog*. (Most disks are $4 each.)

Unlike many shareware distributors, BMUG thoroughly checks each program for viruses, offensiveness, and compatibility with current system software. BMUG disks are available in any combination. You do not need to be a member to purchase disks.

BMUG PD-ROM

This is our complete software collection on compact disk, with over 600 megabytes of publicly distributable software, articles, and other special material. Much of it is unavailable elsewhere.

The *PD ROM* comes with *HyperCard* and our custom stack for browsing the collection.

Among Mac CD-ROM shareware collections, only BMUG offers this combination of highest quality, low price, and free technical support for registered owners.

Glossary

32-bit QuickDraw – a version of QuickDraw which allows the computer to show more than the 256 colors provided by Apple (see also QuickDraw)

Adobe Type Manager – a program for rendering Adobe PostScript Type 1 fonts on your screen

ATM – see *Adobe Type Manager*

alert box – a dialog box which notifies you of some event which is about to happen

application – a program which runs without any support other than that provided by system software

ASCII – an international standard for numbering characters

Balloon Help – a feature of *System 7* which shows a balloon containing additional information about an object

booting up – starting your computer, either through the on/off switch or the Restart menu command

cdev – abbreviation for Control Panel Device

check box – an item in a dialog box which allows you to set an option by checking it

clicking – hitting the mouse button once

Clipboard – the System's temporary storage place for text, graphics, and resources

close box – a small box in the upper-left corner of a window which, when clicked, closes the window

color dropper tool – a tool in the color editors which allows you to "pick up" a color so that you can use it elsewhere

command key equivalent – a key which you push, along with the Command key, to activate a menu option

Control Panels – System 7's Control Panel devices

Country code – a value which tells the System which country you are localized for (see also **localization**)

crosshair – a specific type of cursor which looks like a plus sign

213

CursorAnimator – a Control Panel Device which you can use to keep a library of animated cursors for use in the Finder

data fork – the area of a file where all data is stored, such as the text from a word processing document

dead key – a key which does an action on the key typed after it, such as putting an accent mark over a letter

Desktop file – an invisible file which holds all the icons for the Finder, as well as comments from the Get Info... box

desktop pattern – the pattern, gray by default, which covers most of the Macintosh screen when in the Finder

Dialog Manager – the part of the Macintosh Toolbox which handles dialogs to make sure that everything is working properly

dialog box – an element of the Macintosh interface which usually allows you to make specific choices for an action

document – a file which needs an application to run it

dogcow – the logo of Developer Technical Support at Apple Computer

dpi – dots per inch; the number of pixels in one inch of screen space

dragging – while holding down the mouse button on an object, moving that object around the screen with the mouse

Dvorak keyboard layout – a specialized keyboard layout said to provide more efficient typing

editor – any area in *ResEdit* which allows you to edit a resource

eraser tool – a paint tool which erases pixels

Façade – a program which changes the icon for a floppy disk or hard drive

FatBits – a special view of pixels which enlarges them for easy editing

file creator – the four-letter code for the application which created a file

file type – the four-letter code which represents the type of a file

Finder – the area where you put things in the Trash, copy disks, and do other file operations

FKEY – a special type of program which acts upon a key sequence, usually Command, Shift, and some number key

flag – a special type of variable which can only be true or false, usually seen in true/false radio buttons

Font Manager – the portion of the Macintosh Toolbox which controls how fonts are handled

font metrics – the measurements of a character, which include: the character width; ascender or upper height of a character; and descender or lowermost height of a character

Font/DA Mover – a utility provided by Apple which moves fonts and desk accessories into various files

gray-scale – a color scheme in which every color is replaced by a shade of gray

grayed-out – the term for an item which is disabled

RAM – the amount of memory the computer has to work with

resource fork – the area of a file which contains all resources

ROM – memory which is fixed within the Macintosh and cannot be changed

Script Manager – the area of the Mac Toolbox which deals with handling the international codes

separator line – a gray line which separates different areas of a menu

shibboleth – a catchword or slogan used to distinguish members of a particular group.

Standard File dialog box – the dialog you use to open or save a file

suitcase – a special file which contains fonts or desk accessories

SunDesk – a program for installing color icons on your desktop with System 6

System Folder – a special folder which holds the System and the Finder

system heap – the amount of memory the System reserves for itself

text view – viewing by name, date, kind, or size in the Finder

Toolbox – the area of the Mac operating system which handles all the elements of the Mac interface

TrueType – a new font technology introduced by Apple with System 7

typeface – a font

user interface – see **interface**

version numbering scheme – Apple's guidelines for assigning a version number to a program

watch cursor – the cursor that you see while the Macintosh is busy

zoom rectangles – an animation sequence which is seen when a folder or program opens

Index

Symbols

Colophon:

Zen and the Art of Resource Editing was designed and produced on Macintosh Computers running *System 7*. Type is from the Stone family of faces from Adobe. Body text is Stone Serif 10/14, chapter heads are in Stone Sans 48/49, and sidebar text is Stone Informal Italic 9/13. The book was produced using *Aldus PageMaker 4.01* for layout, *Adobe Illustrator 3.2* for PostScript illustrations, *Adobe Photoshop 2.0* and *MacPaint 2.0* from Claris for bitmapped image preparation, and Andrew Welch's *Snipper* for taking screen shots. The book was proofed on an *Apple LaserWriter IINTX*. Final copy was output on a *Linotronic 300* and *Agfa SelectSet 5000* at Hunza Graphics.

The cover of *Zen and the Art of Resource Editing* was designed with *Adobe Illustrator 3.0*. Bitmapped elements were assembled and separated in *Adobe Photoshop 2.0*. The three-dimensional elements on the cover have been modelledand rendered with *Infini-D* by Chuck Carter. The final cover artwork was assembled and separated from *Quark XPress 3*. Film separations were output on the *Agfa SelectSet 5000* at Hunza Graphics in Berkeley.

Layout and cover were designed and produced by Hans Hansen and Noah Potkin.

Talking: seven steps, eight falls.
Silent: tripping once, twice.
Zennist everywhere,
Sit, let the mind be.

What comes on the Disk:

The disk enclosed with this book has a variety of programs and utilites you can use to complement the instructions found in this book. To use one of these files, double-click on it to open it with *Unstuffit Deluxe* (included on the disk). It will ask you where you want the decompressed file. Tell it where using the dialog and it will uncompress the file for you. Here are the files included on this disk:

- **Read Me First!**: Read this file first for information about the disk.

- **ResEdit 2.1.1**: This is the latest version of *ResEdit*. For more information about using this program, read the book.

- **UnStuffit Deluxe**: This program, from Aladdin Systems, will decompress files compressed with *Stuffit Deluxe 2.0.1*

- **Sample Resources**: This folder contains several more folders, each of which has lots of sample resources for you to use. These resources have been m into the public domain by the authors, and many include Read Me files w information about distribution. If a resource does not have an accompanying Read Me file, you should contact the author for more information a distributing those resources. The different types of resources include cu icons (including color folder icons for System 7 users), color d patterns (including an Escher Desktop pattern that is bigger than 64 and keyboard layouts (including a Dvorak keyboard).

- **Editors for ResEdit**: This folder has three editors you can install into *ResE* Chris Reed wrote the acur editor and the snd editor, and Derrick Schneider wrote the fmap template. For instructions on how to use each of these editors, read the Read Me files which accompany each one. For instructions on how to install these editors, read appendix two "Installing Editors".

- **Programs For Your System Folder**: This folder has two programs inside it. *Keyboard Switcher* was written by Jim Walker, and it allows *System 6* users to have all the functionality that *System 7* users enjoy in handling keyboard layouts. *SunDesk* was written by Frédéric Miséréy, and allows *System 6* users to display color icon families on their Desktops. For instructions on how to use each of these programs, read the Read Me files accompanying them.